C000177057

TO MEET THE FIRST MARCH BROWN

'And now the end is near; we part a space
You to your mud and I to mine — in town;
May Easter find us at the trysting place,
There where the dancing bubbles spin and race
To meet the first March Brown!'

'Green Days and Blue Days'. Patrick Chalmers

TO MEET THE FIRST MARCH BROWN

Geoffrey Bucknall

Illustrated by Aideen Canning

SWAN·HILL
PRESS

Books by the same author:
Big Pike
Fly Tying for Beginners
Fly Fishing Tactics on Still Water
Fly Fishing Tactics on Rivers
Reservoir Trout Fishing
Geoffrey Bucknall's Book of Fly Fishing
Fishing Days
Modern Techniques of Still Water Fly Fishing
Techniques de la Pêche à la Mouche en Lac

Copyright © 1994 by Geoffrey Bucknall (text) and Aideen Canning (illustrations)

First published in the UK in 1994
by Swan Hill Press
an imprint of Airlife Publishing Ltd.

British Library Cataloguing in Publication Data
A catalogue record of this book
is available from the British Library

ISBN 1 85310 474 4

All rights reserved. No part of this book may be reproduced or
transmitted in any form or by any means, electronic or mechanical
including photocopying, recording or by any information storage
and retrieval system, without permission from the Publisher in writing.

Printed in England by Butler & Tanner Ltd.

Swan Hill Press

an imprint of Airlife Publishing Ltd.
101 Longden Road, Shrewsbury SY3 9EB, England

Contents

This book is dedicated to the fishing friends of Upper Teesdale, fine anglers all; Colin North, Bob Oliver, Jeff Sage, Mike Robinson, Joe Tingle and others, too numerous to mention in our Northern fishing club . . . good friends.

Acknowledgements

Over the years I have been given the opportunity to develop ideas and record experiences in various publications, past and present, and I wish to express gratitude to their encouraging editors of those times:

The *Fishing Gazette* (Mrs. Pat Walker, née Marston), *Trout & Salmon* (Roy Eaton, the late Ian Wood and their successors), *Rod & Line* (Dr William Currie), The Flydresser (Tony Deacon), *La Pêche et les Poissons* (Jerome Nadaud), *Plaisirs de la Pêche* (the late Philippe Matthieu), *Fiske Journalien* (Olof Johanssen), *Salmon Trout and Sea Trout* (David Goodchild), *Flyfishers' Journal* (Kenneth Robson), *The Guardian* (Christopher Driver), *The Field* (the late Capt. T.B. Thomas), *Anglers Annual* (the late Eric Horsfall Turner), *Shetland News, Sheffield Morning Telegraph, Kent Life* (Robert Songhurst), *Anglers Mail* (Jerry Hughes), *Angling Times* (Jack Thorndyke and successors), *Atlantic Salmon Journal, Creel* (Bernard Venables), *Angling* (the late Kenneth Mansfield and Brian Harris), *Anglers World* (Len Cacutt), *The Roundtable* (house magazine of the American United Flytiers, *Trout Fisherman* (John Wilshaw).

I am grateful to Dr J. P. Pequegnot for permission to quote from his book *Mouche Artificielles Françaises* and to reproduce his illustration on page 140.

I also thank Paul Canning for reading my MSS with constructive observations, and to his wife, Aideen, for the excellent illustrations. The time to write and fish was unlooked for, thanks to the economic wizardry at Westminster, and thanks, too, to the Grim Reaper for staying his hand; he has a soft spot for anglers.

Chapter 1
An Early Start

That is the only way to treat beginners; to fend off from them where you can, utter discouragement, but not on any account to tell them too much.

Rod and Line Arthur Ransome

Our family, we were Weldishmen. The small stream, the Teise, meandered through our valley. My early boyhood had been one of twitching out small roach on flour-and-water paste. Occasionally I would watch with awe when a farmworker came to the pond with a mighty pike rod, doubled flaxen line tied to the end, and with a roach or frog livebait, he would set about the doom of the 'fell tyrant of the wat'ry plain.' In our neighbouring village, the poet Edmund Blunden watched the great pike by the watermill, and he penned his epic poem which described the miller staring in amazement at the swirl in the water.

Sad to relate, my family left for Suburbia not long after the last war had started, and I was still a roach addict at that time. It is to the late, unlamented Nazi war-lord that I owe my infection with the dry-fly virus, for one of his flying minions deposited high explosive so close to our house that I was able to stroll about in front of the local maidens, swathed in bandages and posing as a nonchalant hero. Authority decreed that the remains of the house would fall down on top of us and that I should return to the village from which I had sprung. Some honest farm-work was the best medicine for bomb-blasted youngsters.

One day, after hours of dreamily watching a red-tipped porcupine quill in the gravy-coloured water of a farm pond and growing bored I strolled down the forstall nearby towards the stream which I knew wended its twisty way through the hop-gardens below. As I came to the river I saw the farmer, whom I knew, performing strange gyrations with a rod. Later I was to learn that he was a dry-fly fanatic. I watched with wonderment as he cast his fly upstream, to fall like thistledown in the shade of the far bank, where plopping circles indicated a fish was rising. Then, suddenly the fish came to his fly, he struck and played out one of the fighting, scarlet-spotted wild trout which the Teise harboured in those far-off days. He recognised me as the schoolmaster's son who was fishing mad, a reputation which haunts me to this day when, on rare occasions, I meet again people from my village. I was one of the local lads who cheered the otter-hunters along on their annual forays along the banks of the Teise. We had swarmed over the wreckage of a German 'Flying Pencil' bomber which had cut a swathe through his hop-garden. This emboldened me to ask if he would teach me the art of dry-fly fishing, for I knew by report that he would allow no other method of fishing on his stream, and he even dismissed the wet-fly as 'block and tackle stuff'.

At this time and place I first mastered the rudiments of casting the dry-fly with an ancient Greenheart rod. The mystery of that thick silk fly line was explained, how it had to be stretched out along the fence and greased. The soaking of gut casts was explained, and, later, the tying of grey duster flies by the light of an oil lamp reflected from a mirror, behind.

Decades later I came across a fishing book which was to be one of my favourites. It was based on the log-book of an angling artist, Romilly Fedden, fishing in Brittany before the first World War. He gave this book the simple title of *Golden Days*. Looking back, those early days of dry-fly fishing seemed to be bathed in golden light in my mind's eye. Autumn was my favourite time. The Teise valley would be filled with the golden light of late summer sun. They would be roasting hops in the oast-houses on the hills above and that most seductive of all smells, roasting hops would pervade the valley. The wild brown trout would be at the peak of condition, eagerly taking the floating duns and spinners before the hard times of winter came along. These fish were the colour of old gold coins but brilliant scarlet spots shone along their flanks like specks of blood.

The Teise was an oddity, a true trout stream in its upper reaches before it became a lazy chub stream in the wealden bed of clay below. Although in those days the old Kent River Board stocked it with fingerling brown trout, the adult fish were truly wild. By day I would catch fish up to half-a-pound but the trick was to wait quietly until last light when the true monsters would emerge from their holts under the banks, the undercut havens where fly could not reach. These denizens were around the pound weight mark. Their

'. . . last light when the true monsters would emerge from their holts'.

quarry were the light coloured moths which flickered over the stream at dusk, and the medicine for these fish was the ermine moth fly or the white upright-winged Coachman. To take two such fish before darkness filled the valley, that was my keen ambition.

I did not realise that I had unwittingly turned myself into a dry-fly purist. I wouldn't have known what that concept meant. As the post-war years passed by, the local anglers formed a fishing club to administer the river, and one day, after one of those magical evenings, our Secretary, Dru Drury and I leaned on the parapet of the tiny stone bridge at Goudhurst. I displayed my catch, and he remarked: 'Of course, if you want to catch big trout you should go to that new reservoir at Weirwood . . .' which dates the year as 1958.

I took him at his word, being the proud owner of a Scott motor-bike. In my ignorance, I thought the only way to fish for lake trout was with the floating fly, that self-same grey duster which was my stand-by on the stream.

As William Blake sagely observed: 'If a fool persists in his folly, he will become wise.' For, as luck would have it, arriving at the corner of the dam as dawn's first light was glimmering over the wall, some trout were feeding on small midges which were trapped in the stickiness of the surface film. The grey duster was the perfect imitation, and within the time it took for that grey light to give way to the rosier luminosity of sun-rise, I had taken a limit bag of fine brownies and thought that there was nothing to that lake fishing business.

Next time I went to Weirwood there came the chill of disillusionment, for a wind was whipping the water up into a good lop. No fish, no fly moved. A friendly angler was bemused to discover that not only did I not fish the wet-fly, I only dimly knew what it was. We sat down together to make me up my first 'team', the Weirwood classics of the day, Mallard & Claret, Peter Ross and Rough Olive. It seemed crazy, to cast these flies onto the water, to watch them descend into oblivion, then to pull them back for hour after hour without response from the fish . . . until there came that very first magnificent tug . . . block and tackle had arrived.

The Teise was rich in fly life. It boasted a good hatch of mayfly. Before the mayfly time the tiny inky iron blues would sail downstream in profusion After mayfly time came the medium olive duns, and, of an evening the ubiquitous brown sedge, and the ghostly white gypsy moths from dew-drenched grass. Apologies to Halford, but a simple dry-fly upbringing doesn't necessitate a knowledge of aquatic entomology. In those early years I didn't need to know the life cycle of mayflies. My mentor went to join the

Great Majority; the club maintained the right to fish, not only on this local farm-stream, but further along the Teise valley. I had grown a home-made aptitude with the floating fly and in those days our trout were free risers. And then Frank Sawyer's classical book on nymph fishing, *Nymphs and the Trout*, fell into my hands, opened my eyes and changed my fishing ways.

Yet it wasn't as straightforward as that, for Frank Sawyer had no experience of rain-fed rivers where the water is of necessity coloured, in our case both by the wealden clay, when it rained, and by the stain of iron ore all of the time. For before the days of coal firing in the North, the Kent and Sussex Weald was the foundry of Britain. The great forest of Anderida provided the wood for the smelting, the iron masters impounded water from our streams into their hammer ponds. They made cannons. And they made the iron railings for St Paul's Cathedral at Lamberhurst, ferried them on rafts along the Teise to its parent river, the mighty Medway. The iron ore was always there, giving water and pebbles a tobacco colour. Frank Sawyer could never have stalked a visible fish in the Teise, watching for the white triangle of its opening jaw to strike against. I knew it would rarely be possible to stalk a seen fish, to pitch a weighted Pheasant Tail a foot or so upstream, to give it a subtle lift to induce the take. No, I needed an altogether different approach.

Artificial sedge fly

Certain books should be landmarks in the progress of the intelligent angler's career. Luckily for me Stewart's *Practical Angler* was republished just after Sawyer's book, with its dictum that the Northern wet-fly fisherman should fish upstream. Somewhere between the two practices, I realised, would lie an effective technique for my stream.

This they had in common, that the fly should be cast upstream. The advantages were obvious. They differed in that Stewart was working with a team of wet spiders of fast, rocky rivers. Sawyer was attacking a visibly feeding fish with an accurately pitched copy of its natural food upon the counterpart of which it was feeding exclusively. The compromise between these two methods was to adopt the upstream approach to a nymphy artificial which could hang in the water so that one could, as it were, fish blind. Hare's Ear nymphs were preferred to the Pheasant Tail because, being semi-buoyant, they would not sink too quickly. Parachute-type hen hackles were later attached to peacock herl bodies to achieve the same purpose. A whole new method was added to my repertoire.

This adaption of Sawyer's method became deadly in practised hands. At first, detecting the 'take' was difficult. True, on occasion, especially when targetting a rising fish, a distinct rise-form was seen and hit. Sometimes the leader would be seen to pull down suddenly as if through a hole in the surface — the classic 'take' as described by Sawyer. Even rarer was that sub-surface 'golden wink' he would perceive on the clear waters of the Upper Avon. The easiest 'takes' to hit were the sudden swerves of leader given by a bold fish darting sideways to catch the nymph. Strangest of all was the instinctive reaction-strike for no visible reason which yet found a responding tug of a hooked fish.

Later, when I came to the classic chalk streams I found that I was very accurate with dry-fly and nymph. If you think me boastful in saying that I always found chalk stream fishing easy, then this was because of a hard taskmastering apprenticeship on a stream which demanded accuracy to a high degree before it bestowed its favours. Remember also how my dry-fly upbringing cut me down to size when first I fished a large reservoir.

One problem was that National Service intervened, during which time I did not fish. I was startled to discover how rusty I was at casting as soon as I returned to civilian life. I had been roped into the village cricket team. Folklore has it that we once skittled out our neighbouring competitiors for three runs and then scored just two to lose the match. After matches the practice nets were deserted. Two of our team would bang golf balls across the square. The wicket-keeper and I would hive off to the corner of the field with a fly rod, and saucer as a target. The old routine came back to me.

The trouble was that when I was fielding at deep cover I could just see the rim of high ground above the valley of the stream. My mind would wander off to capture the murmur of the water, the flies skimming the current, the whorls of rising trout, when a bellowing of 'catch it!' would wake me from my reverie as a scarlet streak whistled past my ear and the Captain's 'for God's sake' would echo round the ground, with only the sympathetic smile of the wicket-keeper as consolation.

It's pleasant to know that the very first flies one uses with success remain as firm favourites for the whole of one's fishing life. Grey Dusters still occupy pride of place in my fly box. It was one of the very first flies I tied with my old farmer friend as teacher.

'I know just the right hackle', he would exclaim. Then we would be pursuing a squawking bantam cock around the yard with a forked stick, until, pinning it to the barn wall, he would pluck a single feather from its neck, the shiny-white hackle with the bold, black centre. His shotgun claimed the rabbit from which the blue body fur was plucked. The entire history of fly-tying was stretched out before my eyes, how country folk would fashion copies of what they saw on the water from materials they had to hand; the traditional silk, fur and feathers which Skues applied to the title of his classical work on fly-tying (*Silk, Fur and Feather*) so many years ago. I need little more for the flies I dress and use to this day.

The other great killer was the Coachman. The upright white wings were a sure marker on the water at dusk. The mayfly was important, there was always raffia around the beans in the vegetable garden. Lower down the Teise valley village anglers dapped for chubb with the natural fly, sometimes secured on the hook with the yellow petal from a gorse bush, but we had to make the classic dry-fly. This was the Straddlebug, a simple affair whereby two Rhode Island cock hackles were palmered down a raffia body and secured by a strand of fine gold wire. It serves me as well today.

And for that important witching hour when it was almost too dark to see, that was the hour for the ermine moth. The tail was made of a tuft of orange wool. The white underfur of rabbit, ribbed with black button-thread provided the aristocratic body, topped off with two speckled grey partridge feathers. The big fish emerged at dusk, the trick being to separate their rises from the hordes of small dace and chublets gorging on midges in the stream. Sometimes the ears were a better guide, for there, up in the deep shadow of the bank, surely there was a healthier slurp to a succulent gypsy hawk moth. And up I would send the Ermine Moth. The rise might be heard rather than seen, and the rod would be bucking to fight a fish which felt heavier than the run of brownies taken in the clear light of day.

The farmer had a well-thumbed copy of Courtney Williams, *Dictionary of Trout Flies* from which came the recipes for these well-loved favourites, Welsh border patterns in the main, invented by that sporting parson, the Rev. Powell. There you are, all you needed was a vice, mirror and oil lamp, plus a well-stocked farm yard and a trusty twelve bore. When you caught the village bus to Maidstone and queued in the one-and-nines at the Granada, then a friendly word with the Commissionaire might coax a tarnished gold strand from his braided epaulette for your ribbing tinsel. Ah, yes, the beeswax came from the hive. The one failure was the early search for amadou, the famous drying agent for flies which, word had it, was simply a dried bracket-fungus from the branch of a dead tree. Innumerable evil-smelling brackets were hacked down from rotting trees, cut into slices, roasted in the kitchen range, all to no avail. Thank God for the paper tissue handkerchief!

Chapter 2
The Structure of the Fly

'The proper fly, properly presented at the proper time, generally brings forth the proper result.'

William James Lunn

There's a notable absentee from this book. I have no intention of describing tackle. The reason is obvious enough. If you care to take down from the shelf any fishing book from the past you will find chapters dedicated to rods, reels, lines, all of which are obsolete. As a former retailer of fishing tackle I know full well that our's is a fashion trade. We deliberately build-in obsolescence so that anglers feel uneasy when, say, new wonder materials are introduced for rod-making. Last year's model is consigned to the cupboard or the attic and the latest affair takes its place. Thus, in angling literature, lancewood gave way to greenheart, then on to split cane, hollow glass and lately carbons in various mixtures.

The basics remain the same. There's one item of equipment which never changes from its basic structure even though inventive minds try to improve on it, and that is the artificial fly itself. The traditional dry-fly, for example, is much the same today as it was over one hundred years ago, and it kills.

There will always be a debate as to who tied the very first floating flies. James Ogden's' scarce book, *Ogden on Fly Tying*, first published in 1879, makes the following claim:

'Some forty years ago, when I introduced my floating flies the love of angling was increasing . . . (this would make it about 1840) . . . by changing my end fly I have occasionally made a cast with a dry-fly. In those days it was said that would scare a rising trout and cause him to leave off feeding. On the other hand, I found while my fly was still on the surface, without a ripple, it has tempted the fish to seize it, after I have been throwing a sunk fly in vain scores of times. These observations were the cause of my introducing floating flies. I found it advisable to use one fly only with a shorter casting line.'

Some believe that the first reference to dry-fly fishing was Pulman's *Vade Mecum of Fly Fishing for Trout*, published in 1841, but either way, we tell that dry-fly fishing proper was probably being practised in the eighteen-thirties and the method found its way into print and onto the fly-tying bench at least by 1840. As to the originator of the classical double split wing structure, again it's hard to be certain who could historically claim the credit. Dr Thomas Sanctuary, a colleague of G. S. Marryat who is generally recognised as the father of modern dry-fly fishing, related how the famous anglers of their day used to watch Mrs Cox dressing flies in her tackle shop in Parchment Street, Winchester. She used to tie 'bunchy wings' from a single slip of feather which sometimes split, and from this Marryat got the idea of the upright split wing.

As to the spent gnat, with its outstretched hackle-point wing, the first example of this I have come across was called 'Gilbey's Extractor' and it seems to have been a spent version of the Red Spinner. It was invented by Arthur Gilbey, Hon. Secretary of the Houghton Club, and it was very popular with members until Lunn's Particular and Houghton Ruby proved more effective.

It was fashionable to deride the pedantry of Halford (*see Chapter 3*) with his insistence of perfect imitation of the natural insect. It was easy, too, to point out that no-one can reproduce exactly the cellular structure of the natural fly with traditional stuffs, silk, fur and feather. Even so, later attempts to copy the translucency of the natural fly failed after a short period of vogue. The most notable attempt to achieve translucency was with Dunne's patterns of silk bodies wound over white-painted hook shanks. Trout obstinately prefer opaque materials, thus proving that they do not always see flies in the way we think they ought.

There came many wonderful inventions; parachute flies with the hackle laid flat, variants with extra long hackles and slim advanced wings, flies with detached bodies, upside-down flies, back-to-front flies, flies with pike-scale wings and so on. They enjoyed temporary, fashionable success, some more than others, but always the traditional dry-fly went on and on. There were some oddities which lasted the course. Dry-fly men on Southern chalk streams were frustrated that trout refused 'exact imitations' during evening hatches of the Blue-winged Olive until George Currel, a tackle dealer who succeeded to Mrs Cox's shop in 1886, hit on the idea of dressing his Red Quills with a body of dyed orange in an attempt to copy the Sherry Spinner, female imago of the B.W.O. He demonstrated this to the young Skues who discussed it in his own books, perhaps unfairly assuming the credit for it. Thus the Orange Quill was born.

The heart of a dry-fly is the hackle which has to have fibres stiff enough to support the hook above the surface film. In the old days such fine hackles came from the necks of cockerels of about three to four years old. As dry-fly fishing was then a minority sport supply was no problem. Today we obtain these 'necks' from two sources. The first is a by-product of the food industry in India, China and the Philippines. They come from young birds and the knowledgeable importers have a huge sorting task to eliminate the rubbish and to classify a tiny number as 'A' and 'AA' capes for the dry-fly. Unhappily the race of knowledgeable feather importers is dying out and the market is filled with necks which are advertised as being of 'A' quality, but which shouldn't even be in the alphabet.

The second source of hackles is the specialised breeder, usually in America, who rears birds for fly-dressing only. The aim is to raise a bird to provide top quality hackles within nine months. The methods of feeding and rearing are kept secret but so much chemical is said to be used that the birds are completely inedible and one would expect them to make clanking noises when strolling about. Obviously such feathers are expensive. They are termed 'genetic'.

Much has been written on how to tell a good hackle from a bad one. In days gone by it was not uncommon to see dry-fly men solemnly dropping flies onto a table from a height of a few feet. They claimed to be able to judge the hackle quality by the bounce of the fly. Good hackles should be long in relation to the length of the fibre, stiff and shiny. In the end though, only experience of handling many capes can give you that 'eye' to judge feathers.

Anglers love a controversy. After generations of dry-fly men had sought stiff hackles my occasional friend, the late Richard Walker claimed to have invented a floatant which was so effective that it made stiff hackles unnecessary. It was a fine floatant, but he had forgotten an essential factor. The purpose of the stiff hackle is not simply to give buoyancy to the fly.

If you watch a trout taking floating flies you notice that as the fly approaches the fish, even from a few feet away, the waiting predator betrays a sense of keen anticipation. Its fins seem to bristle. It rises in the water and aligns itself for the capture. The trigger must be the tiny points of light made by the insect in the surface film and the artificial fly has to simulate this effect. There

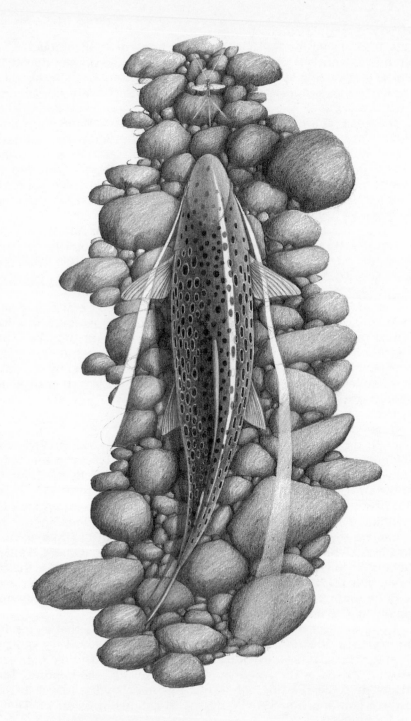

'. . . the waiting predator betrays a sense of keen anticipation'.

was a time when some dry-fly men wound a soft hen's hackle in front of the cock's hackle. The reason is hard to fathom unless it was to copy the 'shadow' of the fly's wings. Skues discussed this in 1897 in an article entitled *More Jottings of an Amateur Fly-Dresser* and he remarked, 'possibly it is to soften down the appearance that some dressers put a soft hen hackle in front of the glistening cock's hackles'. Skues was not adverse to experimentation and he did tie a dry-fly version of the iron blue dun using just a jackdaw hackle, which is soft, I imagine that this must have been one of the first versions of the modern 'emerger dun' which copies a fly on the point of emerging from its nymphal shuck which trout find very tempting during iron blue hatches.

The other quality of a hackle is its colour. Pedantic anglers insisted on using natural, undyed hackles, though quite where they obtained their olive duns is problematical even though I'm told there used to be a breed of bird with a greenish-blue tinge. The argument that the dye-pot dulled down a feather is untrue. Nor does dyeing weaken a fibre. On the contrary, the modern technique of photo-dyeing adds both to sparkle and to stiffness besides producing fascinating shades of blue dun colour. It's strange, too, that the old-timers loved their bi-coloured hackles, the reds and gingers with black or blue dun centres. Perhaps the dark centres gave a forshortening illusion to the fish, making it appear as if the fly was closer to the water, who knows, but I doubt that a Greenwell would fail to catch if its hackle was just plain ginger. Even so you can pick up useful tips from the old and dusty tomes. One or two pedants also spurned the oil bottle, fearing that it would distort colour or leave an oily film on the water. One of them used to waterproof his flies at the bench by dunking them in paraffin and allowing them to dry out in natural sunlight on the window ledge. I tried this; it works.

I have to commit myself now, for although I remain a traditionalist, within the orthodox structure of the fly I found room for improvement. I take as an example that group of upright-wing flies which anglers loosely call 'pale wateries'. I want to avoid that fascinating debate over nomenclature, but bear with me if I point out that there is a group of flies which resemble each other sufficiently to be called collectively 'pale wateries' since they are all, more or less, light olive in colour. Such a group would include *Baetis luteolum/bioculatus*, perhaps the true pale watery, *Centroptilum pennulatum*, the blue-winged pale watery and my old friend *Procloeon rufulum*, the pale evening dun. Some modernists have tried to replace these beautiful old names with atrocities like 'greater or lesser spurwings', a murrain on them.

All we really need to know is that these flies need not be distinguished one from another by the practical angler other than for reasons of mere curiosity. They are all satisfactorily copied by the ginger quill. Although there have been some excellent books on entomology for the angler, for accuracy and plain common sense you can hardly do better than find an old copy of J. R. Harris's *An Angler's Entomology* in which he said, on the vexed question of nomenclature:

'In such matters the hackneyed statement that "the riverside is the only true school for the angler" is eminently correct.'

And now to my own ginger quill. The hook I use is of short shank and wide gape. I prefer the hook with a slightly down-curved shank, currently recommended for buzzers, shrimps etc. Using a brown micro-thread, the first heresy is to tie in a fairly hefty bunch of ginger cock hackle fibres for the tail. These are tied in along the top part of the hook-bend so that they curve downwards to touch the water, to aid buoyancy and to act as a self-aligning rudder to the fly. This places physical needs above imitation which would have the whisks kicked upwards like the natural dun's tails.

The next departure is that instead of using for the body the stripped peacock herl from the 'eye' feather, I use a normal strand of bronze herl with its white root. I rub off the flue leaving the stripped quill, and tie this in and wind it so that the white root of the quill forms a light-coloured knob at the tail end of the fly. The quill can be overlapped to thicken up the body towards the head. The white knob gives the impression of an egg-sac which is quite unnatural, for the sub-imagines it copies do not lay eggs. My excuse is that fish rarely read books on entomology and I have a liking for two-tone effects for flies and nymphs.

The normal ginger cock hackle is wound in, say five turns, but through this I wind in another cock hackle of light blue dun. This hackle is wound in back to front, deliberately splaying the fibres to give an untidy and bristly porcupine effect. After all, this aids buoyancy on knotty, whorly currents at the tails of weir-runs on rivers like the Test. I recall that in the animal kingdom rape is seldom known amongst porcupines.

I dress many patterns in similar fashion, olive quills for example, always obtaining the two-tone effect with hackle and body. Much as I respect Halford's basic concept of imitation, he did overlook the physical behaviour of the fly on the water and the 'exact' part of his philosophy in terms of colour and shades of colour are not so important since we never can understand how a fish sees a fly.

In recent years the split-wing style of dry-fly has lost its popularity simply because amateur fly-dressers find it hard to set on the wing slips. It is probably true that, say, a dun on the water with its folded upright wings, presents only an image of body and legs to the fish below. I recollect seeing a trout on the Test taking medium olives on a regular basis but steadfastly refusing my hackled copy. I had one split-winged olive in my box tied in the same way and at the same time, but with the addition of wings. The trout came boldly to his fly and was duly hurried off this mortal coil. It was an illogical act, but since then I carry some split-winged patterns.

You can also make a case for winging dry-flies for physical reasons because they have a marginal parachute effect, slowing down the descent of the fly. It's no bad plan to hold back a few inches of line when casting a dry-fly, releasing it at the critical moment of leader extension over the water. With practice you can still make a cast with pinpoint accuracy and avoid the heavy plop of the hackled fly with the normal chuck. It's really the opposite of Sawyer's nymph 'pitching' technique, whereby he gave a little tweak to the line to make the nymph curve downwards through the water for a 'clean entry'.

Although it seems sensible to use a stout feather like the grey mallard primaries for winging larger sizes of dry-fly, say size 12 and above, it doesn't suit the smaller sizes and dressers baulk at the delicate starling wing, though with care, starling isn't too much of a headache. I advocate and use jay wing primaries on the smaller flies. The texture is about half-way between a duck and a starling. The colour is of a light, uniform grey, but with a good sheen and it almost has a transparency. For dark-winged flies, coot or waterhen are acceptable to copy iron blues or large dark olives, and they are both fine in texture.

I never cut out wing slips from the parent feather. It is better to tear them out with a smart snapping action, for invariably the quill adheres to the fibre roots, keeping the slips together. An agreeable characteristic of duck quills is that the colour changes from the tip of the feather, which gives a dark iron-blue colour to medium grey in the centre, suiting the olive duns, and on to a light grey for the pale wateries. Some wing-splitting is due to careless tying, that's clear, but older feathers tend to dry out, losing their natural oils, and the tips fly apart. It's no bad plan to touch the tips of these wing slips with a dilute cellulose varnish to hold them together. The fish will never notice.

Typical of the mystical jargon of fly-fishing is the term 'double split-wing', and, indeed, old-time perfectionists did tie in four wing slips, but as a trout would need to be an acrobat, you may safely leave them out and stick to one pair of feather slips. It's easy enough to set wings in the advance position, forward over the hook eye, but this does cause the fly to spin in the air and to kink the leader. I set my wings in the middle of the hackle and fairly centrally in the body of the fly, achieving a narrow splay with the dubbing needle. This avoids the problem and such a fly casts well and rides the water in an upright posture.

There are some gorgeous wing effects achieved with modern materials and methods. Some teased-out yarns give gauzy effects. There remains, too, the old controversy of whether or not to shape wings, either by judicious cutting with scissors or by the use of wing-burning tools. There's no reason why you shouldn't use such devices, they are popular in Belgium and Austria. Nevertheless, the orthodox way, as seen by Marryat when leaning over Mrs. Cox's table so long ago, still works well.

You only need to blend up dubbings in various shades from furs or man-made fibres of various colours, storing them in small film canisters, to have the modern equivalent of Charles Cotton's ancient dubbing bag. And never forget the Lunn dodge of stripping hackle stalks.

Many years ago I dressed some spent patterns for Desmond Berry, then secretary of the Fly-Fishers' Club and I mentioned the problem that most anglers experienced in making flies with split wings. The trouble was that the text books of the time recommended fairly complex procedures with turns of tying thread to be taken around the roots of the wings, then crossed over between them. Mr Berry suggested I should use the club's library to track down the winging procedures of one John Locke, onetime keeper on the Itchen at Kingsworthy, who was renowned for the hard-wearing of the wings of his floating flies. Locke simply tied on the wing slips, splayed them with his needle and supported them behind with close turns of hackle. That's all. No complicated extra turns of silk thread. I have followed this method ever since, taught it to hundreds of 'students' at my classes and demonstrations. It works.

It was also a sign of the times that hackle-point wings were tricky to tie in according to the text-books, which recommended separating the points from the feather and whipping them on, one at a time with too many turns of thread. It is simpler to tie in both hackles together, separating, but not detaching the points from the feather until after they have been positioned on top of the hook. Simplifying procedures is the essence of fly-dressing. There are no critics save the fish!

The simplest way of winging is the rolled wing for sedges, and yet again so many text-books have it wrong so that, after rolling up a wing section like a carpet, the amateur sets it on the hook shank like a pair of wet-fly wings. The section should be tied on to lie flat and as the retaining turns of thread are applied, the fingers fold the wing downwards on either side of the hook shank so that they split and lie flat, very much like the natural insect's wings.

It's comforting to know that the structure of the dry-fly hasn't changed in essentials for one-and-a half centuries simply because it is effective. It's human nature to seek to change and improve, but in the dry-fly the seemingly logical explorations, say into translucency, prove to be unproductive. Of course, as I have shown, there is ample room for variations on the orthodox structures, but inevitably one is forced back to the conclusion, that the oldsters got it right with the dry-fly even if they made a pig's breakfast of the salmon fly.

Dry-fly hackles

Chapter 3
In the Footsteps of Halford

'We believe we know why the Salmonidae take the floating fly, and are, in consequence concerned to try and imitate the natural insect in size, shape, colour and in its behaviour on the surface of the stream.'

An Angler's Autobiography F. M. Halford

The cult of the dry-fly was late in coming to the River Test. Dry-fly fishing was established on the Wandle and Darent long before it arrived at Houghton. The introduction to the *Chronicles of the Houghton Fishing Club* tells us that in their early years club members would either fish downstream with two giant wet-flies or else with the blow line and natural insect, a method much akin to dapping whereby a mayfly or grannom would be carried onto the surface of the water by the action of the wind on a line of floss silk. The strength and direction of wind was critical, and the *Chronicle* quotes that prayer of an ancient Ayrshire minister at harvest time:

'Send us, O Lord, we beseech Thee, a fine wind; not a ratterin'-tatterin' tearin' wind but a huddery-duddery dryin' wind.'

Thus it was that the Rev. Richard Durnford would record in his Test fishing diary for 30 March 1809:

'When the wind decreased the fly went more naturally without the bob and again when the wind was sufficient some fish were taken with the Bob (cowdung fly).'

When that famous keeper, W. J. Lunn began to care for the Houghton fishery in 1887 most members would still be fishing the blow-line method, using a rod of eighteen to twenty feet long. If the journal of Colonel Hawker* is to be accepted, earlier anglers might have fished from horseback for gout seems to have plagued our fly-fishing ancestors, though whether this was caused by bare-legged wading in their youth or the fruitiness of their fine Ports when older is not clear. The Houghton Club was formed by Canon F. Beadon in 1822 which makes it, perhaps, the oldest fishing club in the world. Its history has been kept alive in two volumes of the *Chronicles* and my copy bore the inscription in beautiful copper-plate handwriting:

'To W. J. Lunn with many thanks for much valuable help, Robert P. Page (Editor).'

If it is fallacious to assume that dry-fly fishing began on the Test, there are other equally wrong-headed legends. Consider the tradition that the Test is a gin-clear chalk stream the alkaline waters of which nurtured a wild race of gigantic trout. Should you wander along Stockbridge High Street, cross the bridge over the river at the far end and turn right, along the country lane which meanders by the stream you will eventually be able to quench your thirst at a public house the name of which gives the game away. It is the *Peat Spade*, for the river here flows over deposits of peat. The methane from this peat dissolves in the water and impedes both growth and reproduction of the fish. Early records paid scant regard to fishery management but here and there are references to horse-drawn carts carrying mackintosh-bags of fish from the nearby Avon to replenish the stocks. There's also the suspicion that rearing pools were maintained near to the river for the purpose of growing-on fish. After all, the artificial raising of both trout and salmon had been discovered by S. L. Jacobi who established the first hatchery on the banks of the River Kolle in 1765, in Germany.

In 1905, the then secretary of the Hoxton Brothers Angling Society sent to the editor of the *Fishing Gazette* a diary kept by Lord Glentworth of his fishing on the River Test between the years 1840-2. It makes fascinating reading. First of all though, who was Lord Glentworth? He was one of the Irish aristocracy, grandson of the 1st Earl of Limerick, but he died in 1844 before succeeding to the title, and he seems to have given up his fishing on the Test at Longparish as the dreaded gout was beginning to get to him. He rented his fishing cottage from the redoubtable Colonel Hawker and he was a fishing fanatic. His fishing logbook was meticulous, and I quote overleaf one extract:

---

*Colonel Hawker was a nineteenth century sporting squire who shot with a muzzle loader and fished from horseback. He was a land and riparian owner in the Test Valley.

Where caught	Time	Wind	
Longparish	Monday, June 20th	South	
Upper water	1842		
Weather	Water	Trout	Weight
Cloudy and Showers	High and clear	43	27.25lb

Which gives an average weight of 1.57 lb.

Tracking down the flies from the numbered code book which the noble lord employed, I find that this catch was taken on the following: Blue Dun, Sand Fly, Baillie Fly, Philipps Fly, Dark Apple Green, Kingdom Fly, Orange Dun.

These patterns, popular at that time, were culled from a list of 72 flies listed by writers of the day, Ronalds, Blaine, Blacker, Ephemera and Hofland.

That seems to have been an average day's catch because Lord Glentworth records his best day ever:

'Remarks — Eaton and I commenced fishing at 11 a.m. When we returned to dinner at 3 p.m. he had 31 fish and I 60. He was forced to leave me for town after dinner, but Bowyer arrived and he and I went out about 7 p.m. and at 11 p.m. had caught, he 19, and I 20 fish making 130 in the day. I caught 40 brace to my own rod being the best day's sport I ever had by two fish . . .'

When I fished the place where the Test and Anton join, we had a bag limit of one brace each day. Whereas my heart bleeds for him, Lord Glentworth had some familiar ills to contend with. Thus, when invited to spend a couple of days in a friend's cottage at Wherwell, he complains:

'I never saw but two rises to the natural fly all day. This water was discoloured from weed cutting and I suppose this sickened the fish . . .'

Some things don't change.

There were also some problems with poorly dressed flies in 1841:

'At half-past three p.m. I went out again, and within a space of 200 yards I caught eighteen brace more. I lost three and a half brace of very heavy fish by the hooks breaking at the bend. Oh! Mr. Godden; your March Browns are undeniable, but your gut and hooks are very bad . . .'

Godden seems to have been a local tackle-maker and fly-dresser, probably at Andover, but I have never again encountered his name in angling history. The other curiosity is the frequent mention of March Browns in the diary. I wonder if they hatched in the river in those days or whether the artificial was taken for the grannom? Certainly I never saw them in my own fishing on the river.

Lord Glentworth seems to have eaten trout for dinner or supper every day of the season, not surprising, given the amount of fish he caught and the absence of the deep freeze. It seems also that he waded bare-legged as, towards the end of his lease, he complains of gout and of being afraid 'to wet my feet'. Everything comes to an end, and I sadly record the last entry of 1 September 1842:

> 'Tomorrow I leave Longparish for good, having found the fishing very good, but the cottage too small and as Colonel Hawker means to let the house and all the fishing next year together, it suits me better to give it all up at once. When there is wind, no stream is better. When calm, not a chance of sport.'

On the day he left, 2 September 1842, his very last words:

> 'Sent Charles out with the shoe-net in the morning as I wanted fish to take away. He brought thirty-three, all good fish, one of 1 lb. We packed them all up, got into our gig, and adieu to Longparish. Sorry to go.'

What sort of sport did a lease on the River Test yield in 1842 to Lord Glentworth's rod? Here's a summary to compare to your own logbook:

> Number of days fished: 75

> Average number of fish caught each day: 36.25

Those were the days!

Most dedicated fly-fishermen who take a historical interest in their sport will associate the river Test with the cult of the dry-fly, with the names of Halford, Skues and Mottram. They will know of the classical battles between Halford's theories of exact imitation and Skues' insistence that wet-fly and nymph should play their part. I came to the Test in the late sixties, firstly at the invitation to fish as a guest from a colleague, John Spurway, who served with me on the Council of the Anglers' Co-operative Association. John had a regular rod at Bossington and, later, I also took my own rod there. The highest of our beats adjoined the lowest beat of the Houghton water.

Where these two fisheries meet an old mill lies athwart the river. In days gone by anglers used to stay there. Halford recounts how, on one occasion he was staying there with the renowned Marryat to fish the mayfly. It struck Marryat in the early hours of the morning that the two friends had no artificial mayflies with them, so he needs must wake Halford at four in the morning to help make the flies. In those days, before raffia had been discovered, mayfly bodies were made from straw which had to be well soaked to overcome its stiffness. Old F. M. was given the task of preparing the straw bodies, but not being at his best in the early hours I doubt the two anglers spoke to each other for a day or two.

The old Houghton Club lost control of the water in 1875. They were outbid when the lease came up for renewal. The new lessees also called themselves the Houghton Club, which is confusing, but it is to this group which Halford belonged. In 1892, the former Club regained the fishery they had lost. Halford always used to make light of his literary accomplishments but his sad obituary of his Houghton Club which he wrote in his own autobiography proves that he had a considerable pen:

'But our pleasant times on the beloved Test were coming to an end. Happily we did not know it. Eighteen halcyon seasons had flitted by all too rapidly, and then, without warning, the blow fell! The Houghton Club died suddenly. If one could, on December 31st, 1892 have seen what was passing in the mind of him, who homeward bound with fish bag half-full of grayling, as he crossed the bridge at Boot Island for the last time — a blended picture of present sorrow and past pleasure would have presented itself. Even as he stepped on the Island and closed the wicket — from force of habit — the destruction of the bridge had already commenced on the far side . . . The Houghton Club died when in full vigour. At the time of its dissolution the list was full and with four names down for any occurring vacancies.'

You can feel the pain behind these words and you may guess that it boiled down to a question of money.

When I first came to fish the Test at Bossington, the top beat of which adjoined the Houghton water, the keeper was one of those grand old characters of the river, Reg Dade. He possessed a pair of hollow legs into which one could pour an infinite amount of spirits in the *Boot Inn*, seemingly without any change of mood, except perhaps a slight increase in geniality. My first sight of the river brought disappointment, having been brought up on a diet of phrases such as 'halcyon days' and 'gin clear water'. The river was not gin clear, unlike the nearby Itchen which could, on occasion, fine down to a clear, blue crystal. The Test always had a golden tinge. This may have been due to the silt beds which built up in areas where the current was quieter. Silt is good for mayfly and these hatched in profusion at Bossington.

The Houghton Club, in its golden days before the turn of the century, organised two great fishing parties each year, one for the mayfly, the other to welcome the grannom. The *Chronicle* described those times in this fashion:

'Victorian fishing hut at Bossington'.

'In the leisurely old days of mail coach and po'chaise, men so arranged their affairs so as to come down to Stockbridge at fixed seasons, there to abide for better, for worse, during the time when they were accustomed to have the best sport. They could not, in the twenties and thirties, wait for a wire to tell them that the fly was up, nor could they easily, if they found on arriving that conditions were unfavourable, rush back to London . . .'

And maybe such men would have joined Colonel Sibthorpe, he of the square monocle and hatred of the railways and the Great Exhibition and immortalised in *Punch*, in affirming that 'Holdfast is a good dog'.

I saw the last of the big grannom hatches in the late sixties, saw the last of the dense balls of green egg-sac laden females on their passage upstream. Today I may see the odd sedge or two of a Spring day. It reminds me of the old-time river-keeper's rule . . . 'never cut ranunculus 'till after it has flowered'. What modern keeper knows anything about that? And with that early weed-cut, there goes your grannom.

Thinking of the grannom reminds me that a fly-tying style sometimes makes nonsense out of nature. The grannom is a sedge fly. At rest its wings lie flat along its body. Yet, in the old days it was frequently dressed with upright split wings, like an olive dun, and merely to conform to a Southern chalk stream style of making flies. My own tying had a snuff-coloured body ribbed with fine gold wire. I added a tag of bright green floss to copy the female's egg-sac on some flies. The body and throat hackles were from a ginger cock and the wings were from a slip of speckled partridge wing folded over the hook shank. The natural grannom is an easy fly to copy.

Traditionally, the Iron Blue Dun is a fly of the cold winds of early season. In angling literature the lover of the iron blue was H. Plunket Green who devoted a whole chapter to this fly in his agreeable book *Where the Bright Waters Meet*. This is what he said of it:

'If I was to be limited to one fly for the rest of my life I would scrap all others and stick to the iron blue quill.'

Now there are some flies which, in their season, you could set your watch by, say Mayfly on the Test, March Brown on the Teviot, but my experience of the iron blue is that its coming is entirely haphazard. One of the nicest hatches I saw was at Leckford when that discerning keeper, Ernie Mott, having his back to the river whilst cutting grass, suddenly remarked:

'There's one rising, up by the grill.'

And my companion turned to me, saying,

'He must have eyes in his arse!'

The classic pattern to deal with hatches of the iron blue is dressed on a small hook, say 14 or even 16, with a crimson tying silk dubbed with mole's fur for the body. Some turns of this crimson thread can be left exposed at the tail of the fly as a tag, and then the fly is completed with iron blue hackle and tail whisks. If you wish to add wings, dyed starling or coot or waterhen will serve.

The male spinner of the iron blue is a pretty fly called the Jenny Spinner which rarely comes on the water so that anglers don't bother to copy it. The body of the fly is creamy coloured with tiny circlets of scarlet at either end. I once came across a beautiful imitation of the male imago called a Pearly Spinner, the body being fashioned from a mother-of-pearl material. The female spinner, though, is a far more important fly and it introduces one of the Lunn classics, the Houghton Ruby. Lunn was a believer in the use of stripped hackle stalks for fly bodies. And why not? They thicken up into a nice taper, they show a striated effect like the natural fly. The Houghton Ruby has a body of a stripped hackle stalk, dyed brick red with blue dun hen-hackle wings tied in the outstretched spent position and clipped off at their tips. The sparse hackle is of blue dun cock.

Spent gnats bring home to the angler the importance of copying not only the colour, form and size of the natural insect, but also of its behaviour on or in the water. A scientific study of trout by Frost & Brown determined that trout, in their first four years, recognise their food by its activity. The spent spinners drift downstream, supported by their wings on the surface of the water and fly-tying should be aimed at achieving the same effect, either by the minimum of hackle or else by wing structure. Since occasionally trout are locked on to the spent fly, this is important.

Legend has it that the Itchen was as famed for its mayfly hatches as the Test. I have read accounts of these hatches in ancient fly-fishing tomes, as well as accounts of their mysterious disappearance. Some said it was due to the road dressings of the time, which also passed a death sentence on the Darent.

The two best days in a mayfly hatch are the fourth and the eleventh. I eagerly hunted through my diary of rod days at Bossington to see if they coincided with those dates as soon as the start of the hatch was announced.

The fourth day was important for the duns. It was said that when mayflies first appeared, that trout were reluctant to accept them. I was never convinced that this was true having seen too many exceptions to the rule. It is true that by the fourth day the hatches of the duns are in full swing, and the trout have switched from chasing the nymphs to the surface. With a dry-fly rule such as we enjoyed, the fourth day was a good time to be by the Test.

By a happy coincidence at that time I was introduced to some excellent mayfly imitations. An adept dry-fly man called Taylor had died. His friends knew that he had invented seven deadly mayfly patterns, but the recipes died with him, until one of these companions prevailed on the widow to hunt through his fly-fishing effects. Three patterns survived which I have named Taylor's Green and Yellow Champions, for dun imitations, and a small Black Drake for the male spent gnat. I have killed hundreds of fish on these flies. I now pass these secrets on.

The Green Champion has three tail setae of black and white barred silver pheasant tail fibres. The body is of apple-green floss ribbed with a black button-thread. A shortish badger cock hackle is palmered down the body with a larger one wound in at the thorax behind two partridge hackles, dyed green, which are fixed as narrowly-splayed fanwings in the forward position. The yellow version is similar except that the body floss and wings are dyed yellow.

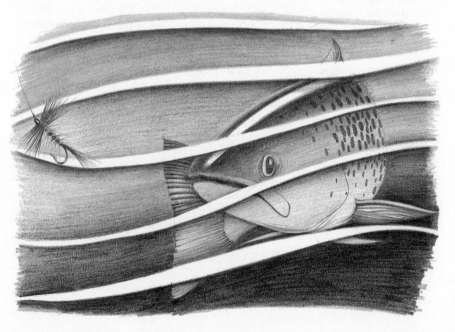

Trout taking dry-fly

A minor frustration in mayfly time is that, if the hatch is very abundant, fish will switch to very selective feeding which they find easier to harvest. Instead of dashing about after active duns which often skid across the surface, they will take the hatching fly to exclusion of anything else. The same is true during a heavy fall of spinner when they will only gorge on the plentiful spent gnats. I never found it necessary to make a deliberate copy of the hatching fly; it was only necessary to clip short the hackles underneath a dun imitation's body.

I have on many occasions found it quite futile to persist with a dun copy when the trout have switched to the spent-gnat, on or about the eleventh day of the mayfly season. For this tactic there was another Taylor pattern, the spent black drake. I have often been told that spent males rarely come on the water. This is not my experience. They outnumber female flies many times over, and gentle breezes bring them onto the river when their day is done. Being a smaller fly than the female, they are pleasanter to fish with.

The spent black drake has three tail fibres from the golden pheasant cock centre tail, a lovely brown and black strand. The body is made of fluorescent white floss, ribbed in one direction with scarlet fine floss, then cross ribbed in the other direction with black button-thread. When wet, the white floss becomes semi-transparent and the ribbings stand out as clear segments of the mayfly's body. Two pairs of black hackle points are tied in flat as spent wings, and a shortish badger cock hackle is wound in for the legs. It is essential for this hackle to be short in fibre as the natural spent gnat, being dead or dying, is supported on the surface of the water only by its outstretched wings.

This is an effective fly at the fall of spent gnat. It always astonished me to see a big Anton fish allow my fly to pass by, then, by making a leisurely circle downstream, the fish would intercept the fly on its return trip . . . as if the fish knew the fly was defunct and had no way of escape. The way a trout takes a dun, hurriedly and fiercely, contrasts with the leisurely approach and sucking down of the spent fly.

These three flies were the legacy from a fine angler. I use them wherever I meet mayflies, from Irish limestone loughs to chalk streams in Southern England. I feel I need no others.

There are many reasons why hatches of fly on chalk streams cannot match the legendary 'clouds' of yesteryear which were sometimes captured by the camera's lens. The quality and volume of water is less. The water meadows have gone. Weed-cutting, if overdone, hurts the grannom in particular and it's arguable that mechanical weed-cutting does more harm than the old-fashioned ways with chain and scythe. Where the 'instant fish' demand is high, the rainbow trout is introduced and its insatiable appetite requires a greater food supply that the indigenous brown trout. It's a catalogue of woe.

This book is not about fishery management, though in passing, were I to manage a chalk stream, I would endeavour to do less weed-cutting to hold insect life and water levels within the stream. I would try to avoid mechanised cutting. I would never stock the rainbow trout. I would enforce a 'dry-fly only rule' for the whole season. I would encourage a no-kill policy with barbless hooks, and, given a long stretch of river, I would replace the allocated beat-and-day for a freer system for my rods . . . but there you are, enough of day dreaming.

The change in the quality of our chalk streams over the last few decades has meant that it's no longer possible to evaluate a dry-fly philosophy like 'exact imitation' in the terms of Halford and Skues. I feel sure that exact imitation was an important factor when fly hatches were so prolific that trout were conditioned to discriminating in favour of a single species of fly at a certain stage in its life cycle. This does still happen on the Test with the mayfly, and occasionally with prolific hatches of blue-winged olive, iron blue and sedge. Many days are not like that, and the angler may well see just a sparse scattering of pale wateries or medium olives. You may spend many hours in mid-summer with scarcely a fly and responsive rise in sight . . . the old dog-days have grown even more dogged.

This has brought about a change in fly selection. Before and after the mayfly anglers pin their hopes on general patterns which copy nothing in particular but which happily attract the fish in a random search for food. Mayfly apart, I could happily pass the whole season with two or three patterns, chief amongst which would be the Leckford Professor, locally known as the 'Cow's arse'. This fly is dressed about face, two hackles, one brown and one white, being wound in at the bend of the hook, and the body, in front, being of rabbit's fur dubbing with a silver rib. It's a strange fly in that it will bring fish up from the very bottom, fish which are plainly not feeding, but lying dormant in deep pools. It takes fish which are rising to sedge, to olives, to pale wateries and to blue-winged olives. It is an effective all-purpose fly with which I have also taken fish in mayfly time. It is effective against bankers, those fish which lie so tight to the margin that you must deliberately drop your fly onto the vegetation, then twitch it off to ride close in, in the shadow of the bank itself. The hackles mask the point to prevent the hook from catching on a stray leaf or blade of grass.

Almost as good is Terry's Terror, invented by Dr Cecil Terry. The tail is a mixture of yellow and orange goat hair, though I substitute a mixture of cock hackle fibres of the same colour because they are lighter. The peacock herl body is ribbed with a fine, flat copper tinsel, and a rich fox-red cock hackle tops off the fly. This, too, is a great assassin on the Itchen and Test.

It's a sad testimony to the degradation of our environment when two or three general-purpose dry-flies adequately replace that golden-days philosophy of correct imitation. True, you may need on occasion an Iron Blue or a Hawthorne Fly, the conditioning hatches still occur, but with diminishing volume and frequency. It is sadder yet that so many anglers and fishery managers accept the situation. It would be insufficient to correct the environmental evils, to eliminate also pesticides and chemical treatment of the land which borders on our chalk streams. Even more deadly is growing fish-greed which demands limit-bag returns for cash spent on permits, which requires the introduction of the gullible rainbow trout into fisheries which are unsuited for it. And the shoulder-to-shoulder jostle of the fly-fishing competition is brought to places which the author and broadcaster Colin Willock once described as a 'Landscape with a Solitary Figure.'

'. . . of the far waterfall'.

Chapter 4
Nymph Fishing on Rain-Fed Rivers

'Only the boom
Of the far waterfall, like doom.'

Tarantella – Hilaire Belloc

My far waterfall was High Force in Upper Teesdale and its gentle roar used to lull me to sleep of a summer's night when I was staying in the old coaching inn a short distance beyond the falls.

I'm not sure who first categorised rivers into 'chalk streams' and 'rain-fed', but it's an intelligible nomenclature. The Tees sucks its water down from the numerous fellside sikes along its course from Cross Fell. It moves through the great Cow Green reservoir, then tumbles over the rugged cataract of Cauldron Snout. A mile or two on Langdon Beck joins the Tees and here there was a savage chemical pollution which wiped out fish and fly life for miles, resulting in one of the largest compensations ever won by the Anglers Co-operative Association, so that the river could be restocked.

In fly-fishing techniques, the last great revolution in the North was over a century ago when Stewart* enunciated the simple truth that it was more intelligent to cast one's spider-patterns upstream than down. The logic was inescapable, that the fish were sublimely unaware of the trap closing in behind their blind tails. It worked. Why change anything?

There was one subtle change, protested by old anglers who fished the river before the moorland was flooded. The Tees

---

*W. C. Stewart, a famous angler of the mid-nineteenth century and author of *The Practical Angler*. He began the technique of upstream wet-fly fishing and is regarded as the father of North Country fly-fishing.

receives compensation water from the reservoir which is a boon in the drought years. This water is drawn from the deeper cold water layer below the thermocline, and this, they say, profoundly limits the fly life, covering the rocks with a slimy algae.

For myself, I think they protest too much, for immediately below Cauldron Snout the Maize Beck brings substantial water into the Tees, water from the sunlit fells along the Pennine Way, and from that point on, numerous contributions are received by the Tees so that within a mile or two of running its course from Cow Green the temperature differential is neutralised. And yet the temperature of the water is an interesting feature simply because when the river is chilled by airs funneling down from Cross Fell, then the fish lie deeper. The upstream spiders fall onto the surface of the stream, are washed swiftly back to the angler without exciting a rise. Common sense tells the thinking angler to use a weighted nymph.

Of course Skues was the pioneer of the nymph, though his patterns were scarcely weighted, were intended to ride close to the surface of chalk streams. Sawyer took the idea further, but again, the faster streams of the North were not mentioned in his writing. No doubt both writers believed the distant waters to be well enough served by the upstream-spider methods of Stewart, for such flies, tumbling in the current, are undoubtedly taken for nymphs by the trout. Again, if they considered the question at all, they probably thought that, as trout in fast, coloured water were rarely seen, except during occasional rises, they were not suitable for stalking and visible attack, the hall-mark of the Southern chalk-stream angler.

I have recounted how I fished for many years of my youth with the dry-fly before Sawyer's book, *Nymph and the Trout* fell into my hands. In those days I was fishing a Wealden stream, the Teise, and so coloured was the water, that only seldom could I cast to a visible trout. The nymph opened up the possibility of 'fishing the water' providing that it could be designed to hang in the water, and this was easily accomplished, either by adding a couple of turns of hen-hackle, or by teasing out a dubbing hair as a collar at the thorax of the artificial. The gold-ribbed Hare's Ear naturally lent itself to this latter treatment. Of course, Northern rivers like the Tees, Wharfe or Swale are much faster and I soon discovered that it was unnecessary to hackle an orthodox nymph, and by judicious weighting, the same effect could be achieved.

Some Northern anglers obviously fish the nymph. In Upper Teesdale I encountered an exponent of the dry-fly and nymph combination who averred that this was the most accurate way of searching for trout which lie close to rocks, where, for example, the typical spider would have neither space nor time to work. Generally though, it isn't an accepted technique, the upstream or downstream spider method prevailing. So it would be a challenge to fish a single nymph. An angler soon learns that the term 'upstream' isn't to be taken literally. The great advantage in fishing a weighted nymph on a fast rain-fed river is that you can chuck it in any direction you like, from straight ahead to straight down.

It wasn't long before I discovered that Frank Sawyer's chalk-stream experiences were not applicable on the Upper Tees. The typical descriptions of the 'wink' under the water when a trout took the fly, or the little white triangle he describes as the under-jaw of the fish reveals itself, or even the 'hole' made in the surface of the water as the nylon leader is pulled down through it, these simply don't happen. The 'take' is either a flurry on the surface or a positive 'bang' on the fly. It's that simple. The fish is either 'on' or 'off'.

I have been going to fish Northern rivers for many years, but once a year I have taken parties of Southern anglers to fish in Teesdale, though most favour the lakes. For a 'stranger', first confronted with such a fast river, the experience is unnerving, the more so if fishing upstream; the problem is that as soon as the line and fly fall onto the water, both come back at a high rate of knots. It seems to be frenetic work, recovering line, keeping in touch with the fly, keeping one's balance in the vigorous current, anticipating a take, then striking and playing the fish. I doubt that either Skues or Sawyer imagined using nymphs in such conditions.

This is only the first impression, though, for so adaptable are the mind and body that within an hour or two, everything slots into place, and it's refreshing to know that an Austrian mountain stream makes the Tees and Derwent look pedestrian by comparison. It is then that you start looking for the likely holding places of fish. The same commonsense rules apply as on other rivers, that fish prefer access to food from a sheltered place where they can avoid fighting the current. Perhaps the artistry of stream fishing is in recognising that such places are not what they appear to be from the tortured surface of the water. True, there are quiet places immediately behind and in front of rocks. Glides and runs are also tempting targets. One of the most rewarding is slightly to the side of a fierce twist in the flow past a boulder whilst another is the quiet run close to the bankside.

The structure of the nymph is both simple and vital. The weighting is two layers of fine lead wire under the thorax, where it forms the hump. The most effective pattern is the Hare's Ear, so much so that I would fish it happily throughout the season. Clearly it copies the March Brown, and also the so-called False March

Brown which comes later in the summer. There's another Tees fly, the Dusky Yellow Streak which it copies, but truth to tell, although we enjoy the philosophy of imitation, the fast-river trout has little time to identify the finer shades of fly-dressing. In the real world it has to grab what's going in the rough and tumble of the current and the imitation only has to succeed in the impressionistic sense of triggering the instinctive feeding response. There are two other flies which are important in rain-fed rivers for which the Hare's Ear cannot answer, the Iron Blue and the Large Dark Olive.

An essential part of this impressionism is to give the nymph a two-tone effect. On the ear of brother hare there are two distinctive shades of colour, a light straw and a dark grey. I use the former for the abdomen, ribbed with a fine gold oval, and the dark fur covers the lead wire of the thorax. A small tuft of brown partridge hackle serves for tail whisks, which I clip short, and almost any brown primary wing slip — say hen — is used for the wing case over the back of the thorax. It's strange that neither Skues nor Sawyer praised the virtues of the Hare's Ear nymph which testifies to their unawareness of the value of the orthodox nymph on swift-flowing rivers.

The Large Dark Olive is similarly structured, using mole's fur for the abdomen and a dark olive dubbing for the thorax, whilst a slip of either slaty-blue waterhen or coot wing feather makes a good wing case. Tail fibres are probably superfluous in these dressings, but the pedant may add a fibre or two from the wing-case material if he wishes.

The Iron Blue nymph also has an abdomen of dubbed mole's fur on crimson silk with dark claret dubbing for the thorax. The wing-case material is the same as for the Large Dark Olive.

When I first fished in Upper Teesdale I accepted local opinion that it was a waste of time to imitate the large stoneflies. These are known as 'mayflies' in the locality because of the season in which they hatch. They are, of course, in the *Plecoptera* family. Some of them are grotesquely huge, up to an inch long. Their appearance gives birth to the famous 'creeper' fishing whereby the larvae are winkled out from under stones in the river course, and impaled on hooks. These beasts are known as 'Jacks' and they have the deserved reputation of taking larger fish.

Although some fly-tying books give dressings for the Yellow Sally stonefly, which is prolific in the Upper Tees, I have never seen one taken by a fish, nor found one in a trout's stomach. I feel sure they are unacceptable to the fish. I recall the legend that Skues was mystified why trout refused some species of fly, like an equally brilliant yellow fly, the Yellow Hawk Dun. He chewed up various flies to determine if it was a matter of taste.

Spitting them in disgust, he exclaimed: 'They all taste the same. Bloody awful!' So whether it is some subtle difference in taste, or whether the bright yellow acts as a warning signal, I can't say. It was pointless to dress copies of the Yellow Sally.

The answer to the problem of the brown stoneflies came to me in two ways. I heard that a young lady fishing in Wharfedale was too squeamish to impale creepers onto a hook, and she tied on a still-water Stickfly against the advice of her companions. She took eleven fish that day in the 'mayfly' season. I mentioned this to my son when we were fishing at that time of year in Teesdale. He had in his box one of those long Pheasant Tail nymphs favoured by Arthur Cove* for Grafham reservoir. He made a great killing with this fly and the fish were of larger than average size.

Trout taking nymph

---

*A contemporary writer on reservoir fly-fishing, especially nymph fishing on the large Midland reservoirs; author of *My Way With Trout*.

I have never been certain about the ethics of using a sight-bob on the leader at some distance above the nymph. As yet, Authority hasn't pronounced on this. I experimented by tipping the leader with a length of extra nylon and superglueing a small polystyrene ball over the knot. This acts as a sight-bob, an asset when fishing fast, turbulent water, and it regulates the depth at which the nymph works. I always felt slightly guilty in doing this, perhaps because it was so effective.

I have a fine memory of fishing the Tees upstream from Broken Way towards High Force. I came to a place where the stream bubbled along, beneath a cliff and in the shade of a coppice. There had been no rise that day, no flies sailing downstream, wings erect. I dropped the March Brown nymph into the head of the run, close to the far bank. The leader tightened into a fine brownie, and I was certain that this was the only way in which that fish could have been taken.

This upstream nymph fishing on fast rain-fed rivers brings home to me the fact that if there's such a person as 'the average angler' who is dissatisfied with his catches, then he should realise that good anglers and raw beginners have one thing in common. They never cease to think about the way in which the current moves the line from the very first second when it falls to the surface of the water. Understanding the way in which the fly comes to the fish, that's what it's all about. I used to tell my tackle-shop customers: 'Two things I can't do. I can't put your fly into the water, and I can't put the fish onto your hook.'

Chapter 5
Border Fishing

'. . . the angler may throw his flies upstream and know less of the art of fly fishing and catch fewer trout than his neighbour who is fishing down.'

The Practical Angler W. C. Stewart

There is only a handful of books which exert influence on one's fishing life. One of these was W. C. Stewart's *The Practical Angler*, first published in 1857.

The change in wet-fly fishing which Stewart proposed was simple enough. The angler should fish upstream. The sub-title of his book perhaps gives the game away . . . 'or the art of trout fishing more particularly applied to clear water'.

I read Stewart's book before embarking on fishing trips to Border rivers. It is curious that over a century after Stewart wrote these words most anglers prefer to fish the wet-fly downstream on the very same rivers on which he used to fish. The reason is obvious. It is easier to fish downstream, throwing the flies across the current. This same current straightens out a poorly thrown line. It brings the flies across the flow. The exciting tugs from the fish are transmitted sensitively on the tight line. Yes, even to this day, the upstream wet-fly angler is a rarity.

I was fascinated by the prospect of fishing Stewart's rivers in Stewart's way and with his fly patterns. I was at first mystified by the way in which his spider patterns were dressed, apparently with the hackle and thread twisted together and wound up the hook shank from half way along. It was curious, too, that his Black Spider had a body of brown silk rather than the black material which anglers use today, and thus it belied its name.

Stewart was a tall man, known affectionately to his intimates as 'the Long 'un'. Two of these angling friends were A. Russel, editor of *The Scotsman*, and A. Bertram, editor of the *Carlisle Journal*. So Stewart had help in preparing his manuscript, and amongst his papers was found a note by Bertram in which he described a 'fair day's fishing' with Stewart as 'twenty-four hours o' creepin' and crawlin'.

It is strange the way that angling literature turns an inclination into a dogma. How many times have I seen it inferred that Stewart stated dogmatically that a man should *always* fish upstream? Here is a note in the *Fishing Gazette* of 5 April 1890 about this great angling sage:

'Our picture seems to portray a cool hand who could fish for many hours on a stretch without turning a hair, land a salmon or lose a trout without emotion, and while devoted to angling, neither be either elated by anticipation or depressed by failure. Not much of a talker but with a good sense of humour. While angling he seemed to possess something like the influence of a fish charmer over the trout. I have seen him, without any attempt to conceal his tall figure, plunging and splashing into the Clyde, in a way that would have frightened away every trout within fifty yards, if he had been an ordinary angler, and yet hooking a trout at almost every cast. Curiously enough, on this occasion he was fishing downstream in comparatively clear water . . .'

It is fascinating to discover the ways in which anglers fished in the eighteen-fifties, and happily we have a record of catches made by these dauntless three in a letter by Bertram during a fishing 'splore' to Aberdeen. It relates:

'Result's of yesterday's fishing:-

Stewart, 45 lb (claims 47 lb)
Bertram, 31 lb
Russel, 17 lb (claims 1 CWT)

Total for three rods, 83 lb. Not such a bad day's sport, eh? It was in the morning that Stewart got ahead of me so far, having swindled me most shamefully as to the water . . . no monsters . . . I had one approaching 2 lb and there were a good many 'off and on' about 1 lb.'

It is clear that Bertram was something of a wag and some contemporaries rated him as the best angler of the three, but it is Stewart who has come down to us as the Apostle of upstream wet-fly fishing, and the writer in the *Fishing Gazette* comments:

'The methods of fishing of which Stewart was the exponent were known to but a few before his book appeared. The mass of Northern anglers had no idea that trout could be caught at all in clear water and bright weather . . . summer was practically a close season. Many a keen angler must have felt the pangs of disappointment on reflecting that when the world was looking at its best, fishing was at its worst . . . Stewart changed all that. He placed within the reach of the practical — not the dilettante — angler the power to make the glorious summer months a season of delight, guaranteeing, in return for careful attention to certain matters of detail, heavy baskets day by day of the best trout, in the pink of condition . . . And this is why many North Country fishers revere the memory of Stewart . . .'

When reading old fishing books I come up against the very same problems as in writing one, which is that fishing tackle is a fashion business with built-in obsolescence. Whichever old classic you pick up, unless you are a collector or masochist, you might just as well flick rapidly through whole chapters which meander through the stock-rooms of greenheart or split cane, gut and horsehair, fibre glass and carbon. Almost before a printed page comes hot from the press, the tackle described thereon can be out-of-date. Yet the essentials remain, based as they are on physical necessities. Stewart said that a long rod was necessary for upstream work and that is just as true one hundred and fifty years later as it will apply sensibly in another century's time, given that the human race will not have wiped out its Northern streams by pollution and abstraction.

On my side of the counter in my tackle shop I frequently encountered the nervous customer who confessed that he was a rank beginner to fly-fishing, and I reassured him that despite its mysteries, its confusing jargon and frustrations, that this time is the most enjoyable in an angler's career. So it was when I was widening my horizons from that early narrowness of dry-fly upbringing with a determination, amongst other things, to follow falteringly in the footsteps of Stewart. The opportunity came in the form of a commission from the now defunct magazine, *Creel*, to explore and write about certain Border rivers, the Whiteadder, Blackadder and Teviot, the last of which continues to exert a fascination on my fishing life. I was to be accompanied by a photographer-chauffeur, John Palmeri, one time racing driver with the Cooper-Lotus team and, in those pre-speed limit days, whose conveyancing of my body Northwards in his huge sports Fiat had a most therapeutic effect on the bowels!

One thing became clear immediately, perhaps highlighted by Bertram's view of Stewart fishing downstream. It makes no sense to fight the wind! If a strong breeze is hammering away, down with the current, then go down with it. It followed that I learned quickly, that downstream wet-fly fishing was not the simpleton's way of avoiding bad technique. The first time this was brought home to me was when leaning over that Teviot bridge below Ancrum over the punningly-named Cleikamin pool. There, below me, was an elderly downstream exponent at work, one hand holding his net-cum-wading-staff, the other winkling a team of flies between the weed-beds below. I learned then, and have confirmed it many times since, that downstream work can be a demanding business which only fools denigrate. The advantages which Stewart cited for the upstream method still hold good. It's worth quoting Stewart on this subject:

> 'The first and greatest advantage is, that the angler is unseen by the trout . . . The next advantage of fishing up we shall notice, is the much greater probability of hooking a trout when it rises . . . Another advantage of fishing up is, that it does not disturb the water so much . . . The last advantage of fishing up is, that by it the angler can much better adapt the motions of his flies to the natural insect . . .'

With these logical arguments, why do so many anglers fish downstream, even despite a contrary wind?

What Stewart didn't mention was the discouragement which is at first encountered and which can only be overcome by persistence. Given a fast Border stream, as soon as you throw the line upstream everything seems to happen at once. Of course the current carries the line back towards you and before you know it, you have line looping between your legs and bellying downstream. The flies are awash immediately and you have no control over them. There's a completely different pace to the fishing. If you do persist you realise that as soon as the line and flies fall to the surface of the stream you have to start raising your rod tip whilst retrieving line back through the rod rings, and this has to keep you in touch with the flies, neither allowing them to be slack and lifeless, nor dragged back at an unnatural speed. In other words, you must know and 'feel' the speed of the current and match it.

You realise, too, that the structure of your flies must complement this. The hackles must be sparse and soft, for it's useless if they are so heavily dressed that they stick to the surface of the water during a good part of their travel back towards you. They must have a clean-cut entry through the surface film so that they pierce it at the very moment they arrive. Frank Sawyer's dodge of pitching a nymph through the surface film by giving the line a smart jerk as the flies and leader straighten over the water is a useful technique.

At the same time, these spider patterns must allow the hackles to open parachute-wise as they come down with the current, which is why they are dressed with a 'kick', that is a thread bolster behind the hackle to force it outwards.

It feels strange to tread the same banks of Border streams where these three famous anglers fished the best part of a century ago. Over recent years the Spring runs of salmon in the Teviot have grown sparser and my friends and I paid more attention to trout early in the year. It was a trick of Bertram's that he would conceal a cod in his fishing bag and then act suspiciously enough in the presence of his friends to tempt the water-watcher to search his bag with great hilarity all round. It seems that a few fish run the Teviot in February; legend has it that they do not go beyond Ancrum. My friends and I fish the Lothian Estates water, renting one of the boathouses close to the river. My logic is that there's a chance of a salmon, though not a good one, but the excellent trout of the river are there in reserve.

This past week, the week before Easter, has been typical Spring fishing. Every day the wind was strong, out of the West, sometimes with stinging rain or hail in its face. Between the tumbling clouds bright sunshine glittered on the turbulent water. It was hard to put a fly accurately onto the water close to the far bank and I was thankful of the trouble I had taken to turn myself into an ambidextrous caster, for, wading down the whaleback shingle banks in the middle of the river, no matter which bank I aimed at, by changing my casting arm the wind would always carry the flies away from face and neck.

I am always astonished at the hardihood of the March Brown fly, for no matter how cold and strong the wind, that fly will always appear, almost on the stroke of noon. And how it wakes up the river! Water which just seconds before seemed devoid of trout, would suddenly break open into whorls of rising fish. For an hour, maybe even two, the hatch continues, for the Teviot is a prolific river. Sometimes the hatch is so abundant that every square inch of water has its floating occupant, and there are intervals of quietude in the rise, when the flies sail down unmolested as if the preying fish pause for breath or are glutted with the turkey-brown duns.

The week started mild but each day grew progressively colder and so did each day bring larger and larger hatches until the Thursday before Good Friday found me at the head of the run just below Nisbet bridge witnessing the greatest hatch of March Brown I had ever seen, with frenzied trout even slashing in the shallow water through which I had just been wading. Within casting reach I

'. . . frenzied trout even slashing in the shallow water'.

had some twenty targets, but no matter how effectively I covered them with a team of wet-flies I couldn't achieve a 'take'. It's a bizarre paradox which fly-fishermen come to accept, that best results often come from the sparsest rise whilst the most promising hatches prove disappointing. On reflection, the reasons are obvious enough. The angler is infected by the excitement of the rise and his anxiety to profit from the situation makes him cast hurriedly, perhaps clumsily, switching targets. It is hard to fish calmly and accurately at such a time. Then the fish themselves are locked-on to a certain natural fly in a certain behavioural state, say floating duns. Each fly overhead enhances the image so that anything 'out of synch' is rejected. The ideal would have been for me to go below the fish, casting a dry-fly up above them, but the very strong downstream wind ruled out that obvious tactic.

This even brought home to me the classical argument, 'Imitation versus Presentation'. It's not too difficult to copy the March Brown. I dress two versions for wet-fly fishing, the standard winged fly for downstream work, the hackled spider for the upstream attack, tied with a 'kick' to give it more semblance of life when tumbling back to me in the current.

The dressing of the March Brown goes back for centuries. The body is made by dubbing yellow silk thread with the brown hare's fur — and it must be a true mustardy-brown colour without the contamination of bluey-grey underfur. Normally the tail and hackle are from the brown partridge hackle, but although this suits well, it is a fairly coarse feather and I prefer to use a strongly freckled Cree hen or cock hackle if I can find it. The wing is also speckled, the slips being taken from the well-marked feather of a partridge tail. It's not an easy feather to work with, being prone to split and it's vital to use slim feather sections and tie them in so that they lie close to the body of the fly. A gold rib, even a gold tag, adds attraction to the fly. The spider version is straightforward enough, the wings being omitted and the hackle wound as a collar right round the hook shank. The 'kick' is made by forcing the hackle fibres outwards, at right angles to the body with two or three turns of tying thread right behind them as a shoulder.

Two other March Brown artificials work well on Border streams. The first is a weighted nymph to be pitched into deep water or fast runs when no natural fly is on the water. I wrap a layer of fine lead wire onto the hook then shank, dub the hare's ear. You will notice that it has two shades of brown, dark and light, which can be used to achieve a two-tone effect, using the light fur for the abdomen and the dark for the thorax. A tuft of the speckled hackle is tied in as a beard under the thorax, the same feather serving as short tail whisks, and a strip of the partridge feather over the top of the thorax serves as the wing cover. The abdomen needs a fine gold ribbing for extra effect.

Of course that leaves the dry-fly which is deadly on the Teviot even on fiercely cold days. The version I have used for over two decades is the 'Fast Water March Brown'. The body and tail are the same as the wet-fly, but the hackles are of either a well-marked Cree cock or brown partridge hackle in front of two stiff white cock hackles. The March Brown is not a gentleman of calm chalk-streams. It enjoys the rough and tumble of the torrent where the artificial has to float well and to be visible to the angler in a confusion of broken water. This fly manages both things superbly.

The other two important flies of this Spring fishing along the banks where Stewart passed are the Large Dark Olive and the Iron Blue Dun. The former is efficiently copied by that age-old favourite, the Blue Dun with mole's fur finely spun onto yellow silk for the body, blue dun hackles for tail and throat and grey mallard primary wing slips for the wings. It seems strange that whereas there are few choices to copy the Large Dark Olive the Iron Blue has myriads of imitators. It comes down to personal choice in the end and I doubt you can do much better than the Snipe & Purple.

I rarely tie on a Snipe & Purple without sparing a thought to another renowned angler of the past, T. E. Pritt. Although not such a radical book as that of Stewart, Pritt's *Yorkshire Trout Flies* had a strong influence on my North Country fishing. The Snipe & Purple was a favourite fly of Pritt. The dressing is very simple: wings hackled with the feather from the *outside* of a snipe's wing, body of purple silk. And though very simple it is important to get it just right. My friend Oliver Edwards, superb fly-tyer from Yorkshire, will remind you sharply, as he did to me, that no other feather will do. As for the body, the purple tying silk from Pearsal will suffice, though you may open the turns if you are a pedant and tie in the hackle with a kick as described earlier.

As for T. E. Pritt, a passing tribute from the *Fishing Gazette* of 21 September, 1895 proves that he was no slouch with a fly rod, and I quote from his obituary, for he died that year:

> 'He can throw a long line with either hand, though as a rule he casts with his left owing to an old injury to his right shoulder. This peculiarity, coupled with an enormous landing net shaft familiarly known as a "weaver's beam" which he insists on carrying in spite of jibes and flouts (wonderful stories are told of futile efforts to get it into a railway train) and the omni-presence of his dog 'Tulip', an animal described by a local

Natural March Brown and the angler's copy

hand as "well-nigh bursten wi' sense" make Mr. Pritt a
noticeable figure on any water.'
When I opened Pritt's book to check the exact wording of the
dressing of his fly, given above, the Dark Snipe, to give its old
name, I was struck by his dedication 'to a host of Yorkshire anglers,
good fellows and good fishers all, and in token of my unbounded
admiration for the beautiful rivers and valleys of the County'.

In the company of two good fellows from the Yorkshire fly-fishing
community I was conducted to fish a stretch of that admirable
river, the Wharfe, where Pritt once held sway with his gigantic net.
Now, these two fishers were also faithful disciples of that
immaculately stylish Yorkshire batsman, Geoff Boycott. On the
drive to the water I was inundated with hero-worship; such phrases
as 'poetry in motion' or 'should have captained England' being
passed about with abandon, notwithstanding that they knew I
came from that not inconsiderable cricketing county of Kent — and
from the proper side of the River Medway at that! On the way down
to the water we happened to pass by a place where they were
slaughtering pigs. And as we passed by, the humane killer
exploded with a sharp crack, followed by the last despairing squeal
of the stricken animal.

'What's that?' enquired one of my startled companions.

'Sounds like Boycott facing Underwood,' I told him.

There are many other fine copies of the Iron Blue. The Waterhen Bloa' is favoured by many, and the true pattern boasts a body of dubbed water-rat fur. This little beast, for which I have much affection, boasts a fascinating pelt, the surface of which is a polished dark brown but with a dark blue underfur. The fur is impervious to water and so it has a sheen to it when submerged. Modern dressers use mole instead of the stipulated dubbing and if that spares my friends from the *Wind in the Willows* then I am grateful for that. The legs of this fly are from a hackle feather from the inside of a water-hen's wing.

A curiosity is the inclination which Border trout have to take flies with a bouquet of orange in their make-up, and this is especially true of copies of the March Brown. Pritt noticed this and one of his own March Brown flies calls for the hare's ear fur to be spun onto pale orange silk. That old favourite, the Grouse & Orange kills well on the Teviot and I rarely lack it on my team when fishing in Upper Teesdale. Yet, when finally deciding for a wet-fly team for Spring fishing on the Teviot, it would be those three favourites: March Brown on the point, Snipe & Purple for the middle dropper and Blue Dun on the bob. That covers the three natural flies one will encounter on the river at that time of year. If an upstream wind did happen along, then the dry-fly would be an option, favoured, strangely enough, by the odd sea trout.

Chapter 6
Fishing the 'Big Cow'

'Fish take all sorts of baits more eagerly
and freely, and with the least suspicion,
when you present them in such order and
manner as nature affords, and they are
used to take them.'

The Driffield Angler Alexander Mackintosh

The 'Big Cow' is the uncomplimentary name for the Cow Green
Reservoir in the High Pennines. This lake lies plumb across
the border between Yorkshire and Durham, and at 1,600
feet, well above the heather line, it is probably the highest large
lake in the country. The River Tees flows in at one end of the lake,
and at the opposite reach it tumbles out over that spectacular
cataract, Cauldron Snout.

Cow Green is a statistician's paradise. The reservoir impounded
770 acres of water, the same area as Bewl Water in Kent, but
whereas Bewl is a series of convoluted bays and channels, Cow
Green is an open panorama of wind-scoured bare banks. Bewl is
visited by thousands of anglers each season, but during the five
years in which I was a syndicate member at Cow Green we barely
sold a thousand day-tickets. The reasons are two-fold. The lake is
remote and the weather can be severe. The trout are truly wild, the
lake's population being renewed only by adult fish spawning in the
sikes which fall into the lake from the steep fells.

I love to fish in wild places. My own love affair with Cow Green
began when I was invited to give a fly-dressing demonstration to a
Yorkshire club. The Secretary, Mike Robinson, a fine angler, invited
me to stay over to fish this lake in Upper Teesdale. Ascending the
valley of the Tees above Barnard Castle is akin to going up a
staircase with trout lakes on either side. Lower down the valley,

comparatively speaking, are the rainbow-stocked reservoirs of Grassholme, Hury and Selset, with a smaller lake, Blackton deservedly reputed to hold large brown trout. A step or two higher and you encounter the unstocked reservoir of Balderhead, the deepest of the Teesdale lakes, being a savage gash in the landscape. Between Balderhead and Blackton the formidable Hannah Hauxwell lived in her decrepit farmhouse. I would give a friendly wave to this white-haired lady as I strolled along the dam wall at Balderhead, little dreaming that she would become a famous media-personality.

Then comes the top stair, the impressive Cow Green reservoir. This place gets its name from the old days when Scottish drovers, bringing their cattle to Southern markets, rested their beasts overnight on grasslands which were protected by the steep fells. There, between Widdybank Fell and Meldon Hill, the drovers built a hut where today Lodgegill Sike finds its home in one of my favourite fishing bays. The Drovers' Hut remains, and the curly-horned Swaledale sheep moodily crop the wiry cotton and quaking grasses of the moorland. It is a lonely place. Many a day I've been the only angler. I loved to watch the huge cloud shadows racing across the purple fells.

The reservoir was created in 1970. There was opposition to the flooding of the valley, not least because botanists feared for the survival of the rare Spring and Autumn Gentians, Alpine plants which flower nowhere else in Britain. Threatened colonies of these plants were moved and protected, so much so that today they probably attract far more admiring glances from visitors to the Nature Trail than in the days before Cow Green, when the valley was only visited by small numbers of knowledgeable botanists.

The land surrounding the lake is of heather and moorland grasses. A deterrent to the casual angler, this rough terrain is fatiguing to traverse, much like walking through barbed wire! Here and there the unknowing visitor will boldly place his foot on the comfortable-looking sphagnum moss which is invitingly green and friendly, but he will suddenly plunge down into several feet of icy-cold water.

Although the surrounding land is peaty and one would expect the water to be acidic, with little fly life and stunted growth of the wild brown trout, the strange thing is that the weights of the fish have increased during the last few seasons which I have fished there. There was a succession of mild winters and when it was expected to see a sheet of ice across the lake, instead friends witnessed the dimpling of trout rising to fly in February. A problem was that these have been good years for the trout to breed in the

Tees and the sikes so that it was necessary to fish through a host of youngsters before latching on to a worthy opponent.

Normally winters are so severe that only this hardy race of trout survive. There are no other fish in Cow Green save a race of bullheads, examples of which I often find in the stomachs of the native trout. Although the surrounding landscape is harsh, of hags and peat bogs, by happy coincidence the lake lies across limestone deposits which give the water a pH of 7.2, and this means a fairly rich fly life with consequent reasonable growth rate of the native trout.

Even so, Cow Green does have its own weather, quite unrelated to the dulcet tones of the weather forecaster's announcements for the dales below. You can go upwards from golden sunshine at Barnard Castle suddenly to plunge into a dense mist at the lake. This same mist, like those described by the Lakeland poets, fills your soul with deep despair, for it blankets out all sound, cocoons you in cotton wool, destroys all sensation of direction as if you were the only person left it the entire world. The plaintive voice of the curlew disappears. It is little wonder that anglers from the towns of the North-East flock to the stocked reservoirs lower down the valley, with the succulent, lush meadows and easily-caught rainbow stock-fish.

The contrasting scene is when the prevailing South-westerlies scream down the Tees valley, bringing the squally showers of stinging rain. The wind whips up such a strong 'sea' that it becomes necessary to lean against its buffeting until the mouth of the Tees is reached where the river enters the lake at the far end. There, the river may be crossed by rock-hopping unless the river is swollen by rain. The sheltered far bank may then be fished comfortably back towards the dam. Forty minutes of stiff walking gets you to Tees' mouth which is another deterrent to slothful fishermen from the South who are used to gentle strolls from convenient car parks to expectant rainbow stockfish.

I must admit that I was devastated by the harsh reception I received at my first visit to Cow Green with that habitué of the place, Mike Robinson. Mike was never so happy as when the rain was coming down like stair-rods, and when I complained, he airily answered: 'Oh, there's many folk in the cemetery who'd like to change places with you!' And it was Mike who showed me the trick of turning away from the water, to make the cast towards the hills behind, then, with a smart turn, to flick the line onto the water.

It was amusing, too, as Cow Green attracted the occasional visiting reservoir angler from the South, to watch this man plunge into the water to his wader-tops, in Grafham or Rutland style, where he would stay rooted to the spot, throwing a lure as far as he could, probably with a sinking line. Cow Green has to be fished like a river. The local anglers fish fast along the bank, rarely wading, but walking a step or two after each cast to put a curve into the line, then retrieving the flies along that curve. Only occasionally is it necessary to throw a long line, and many fish fall victim to the bob-fly when it is worked on the surface from the rod-tip and close to the bank.

For those who take an interest in entomology the rise in altitude, though quite moderate, means that there are less species to interest the fish, and some of these are different to flies which are met lower down the valley. The small black buzzer is the most prolific insect at Cow Green. It hatches throughout the season. I have been on the far side of the lake when, around mid-day, the wind has moderated to allow wind-lanes to form from one bank to the other, and in the shining pathway of light, even far out, I could see masses of minute black dots as these buzzers hatch, but are unable to escape the oily-type of water which forms in wind lanes. Then big fish would be humping in the wind lanes right across the lake. These fish are a phenomenon of the water, rarely being taken from the bank. The enthusiasts of the British Fresh Water Biology Association, who monitor the fauna of Cow Green, tell us that they see these larger trout ascending the sikes in the Autumn, to spawn. The assumption is that when a Cow Green fish reaches a certain size it is able to prey on its smaller bretheren, and then becomes almost entirely cannibal in its feeding habits. This is why it's rarely taken by the bank fly-fisherman. Yet, when the water is smothered in black buzzers these fish cannot resist the invitation to partake of the feast. Alas, even then they feed tantalisingly far out, for boat fishing is not allowed on this wind-swept water.

I took one of these larger fish, a buttercup-yellow trout of 2½lb. This fish accepted a dry size 14 William's Favourite which is an admirable copy of the small black gnat. It was a magical morning when the mist over the water was changing into a golden haze as the sun began to burn it off the fells. As it slowly cleared it revealed a pleasant ripple and a small group of fish taking black buzzers in front of me. On my first cast my fly was eagerly snapped up by one of these fish, and I was immediately broken on the leader loop. I quickly made good the damage and, on recasting, I hit another of the shoal which soon revealed itself as a bigger trout than the run-of-the-mill fish we take from the bank. As I never carry a net at Cow Green I had to gently play the fish to the point when it was turning on its flank, and then I slid it to the shore between the rocks.

'. . . a buttercup-yellow trout of 2½lb'.

On another occasion, fishing along the far bank in September, I recollected the story that large fish collected at the mouths of sikes, ready to run-up for spawning. 'A likely tale,' I told myself, but a tactical choice is better than no choice at all. Having seen the odd water-beetle at this lake, I tied on my Jack Ketch pattern as I approached the mouth of one of the sikes, a place we call White Spot Sike. The Jack Ketch, having a weighted body of mixed dubbing, a silver tag and a long black hen hackle, is an excellent water-beetle imitation. Casting it up into the dark pool where the beck runs in, I had just started a slow retrieve when the fish hit my fly. Lifting the rod I expected to bring a normal Cow Green trout to the surface. Instead the rod pulled down and bucked to the surface of the water, and the hook hold gave way. Jack Ketch was a notorious hangman of years gone by, but on this occasion his noose collapsed.

The Heather Fly comes onto the water in high Summer. This is a black beetle with bright red legs. The Kate MacLaren is good medicine, but dressed with a bright scarlet thread which is allowed to shine through the sparse black dubbing. I can never fathom the Heather Fly. Sometimes it is eagerly taken by the fish, during which rise you can make a good killing. Other times I have watched with astonishment as the wind has drifted struggling beetles across the water without the slightest interest being shown by the fish.

The Heather Moth is important in these Pennine lakes. It is interesting how even modest increases in altitude change the habits of species. In the lowlands moths are nocturnally active, but where food is scarcer in the upland regions moths are not only active by day, but their choice of food is wider than their lowland cousins which restrict themselves to a single plant item. There are probably two or three types of upland moth at Cow Green, but they are similar in colouration and size, so that a simple artificial, which, unsurprisingly, we dubbed the Heather Moth, manages to copy all of them. A body of cock pheasant tail, palmered lightly with a glassy light blue dun cock hackle pinned down with a fine wire rib, that does the trick. Though limited in the number of species, upland moths can be prolific, so much so that my son would often kick them off the grass to induce a rise by wind-driven groundbait!

We also encountered two distinctive species of Cranefly, the daddy long-legs. One was consistently refused by the trout, and that was a smaller version with an attractive purple body. The larger brown one was as popular at Cow Green as its counterpart was on any water you would care to fish for trout.

For a visitor from the South, someone who is used to the leisurely rise of the stocked rainbow trout, the speed of the 'take' by wild trout in hill lakes beggars belief. On my first trip, having missed innumerable fish — and they never come twice — I asked of Mike Robinson:

'Just when do you hit 'em?'

'A couple of seconds before they rise!' came the unsympathetic response.

And even now, the first day of an expedition to the 'Big Cow' is one of frustration, though from the second day on my reflexes begin to gear themselves to the speed of the rise which my grandfather would have recognised.

Cow Green

There is a legend perpetrated by some angling writers that trout in upland waters have such a limited food supply that they take the fly without discrimination. This is plainly untrue. There are long dour periods at Cow Green. It is noticeable that when flies are not coming onto the water, then the artificial fly also fails (worm fishing is allowed on many Northern reservoirs). It is true that although exact imitation in the Southern chalk stream philosophy is pointless, there has to be a practical relationship between fly and artificial. Hence the small black midge can be copied equally well by, say, Black Pennell, Black & Peacock Spider, Teal & Black, Kate MacLaren amongst others.

Patterns for the Heather Moth and Heather Fly have been discussed. There's an occasional appearance of sedge, and the Soldier Palmer is successful as a bob-fly. On occasion, frankly attractor-flies work, say Silver Invicta or Dunkeld, perhaps because of the bullhead population.

There is a relationship between lakes like Cow Green, where the bleakest of days produces a rise, and the rare balmy days do not, and the windswept lochs of Orkney, Shetland and Caithness which I discuss elsewhere. There are also differences, for although I have taken odd fish on Grouse & Claret at the upland lake, it is not first choice, whereas it would be North of Inverness.

I suppose that if the Angel of Death drew up to me and offered me one more fishing day before he whisked me away, I think I would take Cow Green, but not if I could see one tiny dot on the far bank. Then I would join my friend Mike Robinson, who, on seeing this one morning, exclaimed:

'We'll have to move on one day, Geoff. The place is getting too crowded.'

Chapter 7
Where the Wind Rules

'It is the old wind in the old anger . . .'

On Wenlock Edge A. E. Housman

It is axiomatic that a column of air moving across an expanse of water will have dramatic effects. If the water is deep enough to stratify thermally in summer so that a layer of warm water virtually floats on top of a deep colder layer, then the two layers together are tilted towards the windward side. The warm, upper layer will be like a slice of Cheddar cheese with the thin end of the wedge under the lee shore. It's amusing to walk around such a lake on a sunny day in summer, to put one's hand into the water on the opposing margins and to remark on the considerable variation in temperature, but swimmers have long known of the pitfalls of the widely differing temperature layers.

Carp anglers have taken temperature stratification into account with their prey, which generally loves to bask in warm water. The effects in trout fisheries are more complex, and having seen underwater photographs of trout swimming well below the thermocline, I am sceptical of the theory that they do not inhabit these chilly areas of a lake where oxygen is said to be low. The effects on fly life are complex. It has been said that until the overall temperature of a deep lake begins to increase after the winter chills, that insect life is dormant. As trout recognise food by its activity, at least in their earlier years, then little or no insect-feeding takes place.

When the margins warm up by sunlight, then of course insects become active and fish feed on them. The deep, cold water layer remains quiet. An angler doesn't need to be told this, he sees the trout rising in the comparatively shallow water and he sees the flies hatching which motivate the rise.

The wind is important to anglers in another way. When the surface of the water is calm the surface film is both sticky and strong, so much so that the feebler aquatic insects which need to hatch into the open air, they cannot break through. They are literally trapped in the surface film and fall easy prey to patrolling fish which harvest them in a leisurely way. The fruitful evening rise to the buzzer pupae is the result. Unfortunately, the angler's wiles, his glittering leader and fly-wake are all too visible to the wary fish.

The wind springs up. The surface of the water is broken. The buzzer pupae hatch quickly through the film and the whole momentum of the rise increases, with fish being far less able to discern the difference between artificial and natural fly. The best of both worlds combine when fishing along the edge of a ripple, for here, just a yard or two inside the area of broken water, pupae are slower to hatch but there's enough gentle commotion to disguise and conceal leader glitter and the wake of the fly.

The cold-water layer in a deep lake in summer is a mystery to me. Theoretically, a trout would not want to be there. The oxygen content is low, and it becomes lower as summer progresses simply because the rain of detritus from above uses it up. It's not until the equinoctial gales of autumn mix up the temperature layers that the deeper places are 'unlocked'. Yet this is all theory because divers see fish below the thermocline and great trout are taken on the deep reservoirs by trolling with lead-core lines. In the end we must agree that fish are contrary critters and they don't read the text books. What is strange about the very deep places is the lack of change throughout a season, and from night to day. Neither light nor temperature change except within narrow limits, yet charr are at home there in lakes like Windermere.

When fishing from the bank of a wide lake it's comfortable to have the wind blowing from behind. Some experts aver that best results are gained from fishing into the wind. They cite the obvious reason, that food is blown into a windward shore, and this makes sense. At first, the idea of freezing-cold water welling up from below the tilted thermocline on the lee shore, is discouraging, especially when you feel its chill through the waders. The fish still don't read the rule books! These lee shores on summer days often provide excellent sport, which is fortunate, given the assistance which the friendly breeze gives to poor casters. The contrary is true, for I rarely do well when trying to push a line directly into the teeth of a strong wind on a windward shore, and I hate it if the force of the breaking waves is eroding the bank away into great muddy smears in front of me. It drains away my confidence.

'. . . wild and high places'.

Obviously an angler doesn't need to be a scientist, but a basic knowledge of the physical structure of fisheries helps to develop artificial flies. The strong molecular wall of calm water gave birth to the Suspender Nymph which copies the buzzer pupa when it is struggling to break through the surface film. The modern dressing depends on a tiny ball of buoyant polystyrene to keep it in the film, though I prefer a collar of hackle clipped back to make a stiff ruffe around the neck of the nymph.

The wind rules in wild and high places. Thus it was that I went to fish the River Whiteadder in July, only to find this favourite river so low and clear that fishing was out of the question until the last hour of daylight. Instead, I went up into the Lammermuir Hills to fish the local lochs, that is the Whiteadder and Watch reservoirs.

The day on Watch was one of a strong gale. As I worked along the bank, so did the wind grow stronger and stronger, so strong in

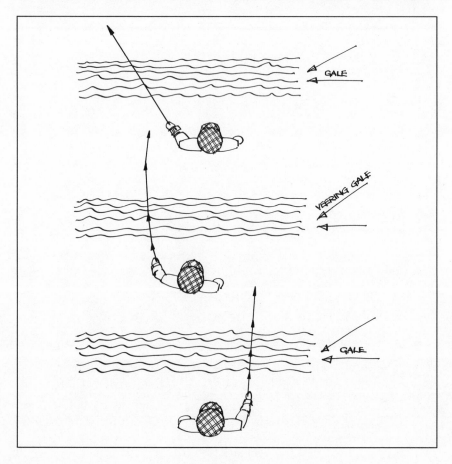

fact that I would have had to give up, had not a strange casting technique come to my aid. Imagine it, the wind howled down the valley, thundering into my right ear, and the rod itself was forced into a bow. The water in front of me was pushed up into high waves, coloured brown with whipped-up silt from the eroding banks, and crested with white foam.

At first I thought a roll-cast would suffice but the gale simply tore it along the bank. Then I tried a double switch cast which is simply a single-handed version of the Double Spey. That wasn't much better. Another short-handed overhead cast slapped the flies into the back of my coat, and that is how I accidentally solved the problem, for I switched the rod to my left-hand to keep the flies safely down-wind, but as the next cast didn't go out too well, I immediately transferred the rod back to my right hand and hit a roll cast. To my pleasure and surprise, the line rolled out straight across the wind for about twenty-five yards. I improved this distance as I progressed, repeating the routine. It was also very safe.

So, there you are, the routine was to pull the line up from 'below', then a left-hand overhead cast put the line in front. This need not be either a long or even tidy effect, but the line, leader and flies are then in the right place to roll-cast straight across the wind. The changeover from left to right hand needs to be done fairly quickly to stop the wind blowing the flies out of position. And you must use a double taper line, as with all roll casting.

It is strange that I have fished for many years in wild and windy places without hitting on this casting routine. It reminds me that the great master of the dry-fly, Frederick Halford, could never straighten his leader into a head-on wind until his companion, Marryat, showed him how to cut down the rod-tip to the surface of the water, and since Halford related this incident, generations of fly-fishermen have used this 'storm-cast' to overcome the difficulty. Even that method, though, will not cope with gales which sweep along the banks of lakes in the high country.

In fly-fishing, at any rate, there's no truth in the old truism that a little knowledge is a dangerous thing. This 'little knowledge' is often just plain common sense, one of the best examples of which is that the wind will obviously carry terrestrial insects from the land onto the water. This is typified by the Daddy Longlegs, especially in Autumn when the females are searching out rain-softened earth through which they can push their egg-laying pointed rear-ends.

The spent females are then carried onto the water where they are eagerly anticipated by patrolling fish. Fishing the Daddy is exciting. The trout takes it with an angry swirl, sometimes tail-slapping first to drown it. A good pause is necessary before the hook can be set.

The Isles of Orkney are renowned for high winds and record gusts once carried away the best part of a chicken farm. One day, when the wind was tumbling the clouds across the sky and the rain was coming down sideways, it was obvious to me that going out in a boat on the wide expanse of Harray Loch would be a hazardous enterprise. I chose to visit the smaller Hundland Water. The wind howled between two low hills at the far end of the water, but right up against the lee where the water was shallow there was a quiet place. Here the wind and water met in a pleasant ripple, which was broken by the occasional whorl where a brownie intercepted a Daddy.

Daddies are easy to make. I concoct two patterns. The first is bushy, dressed on a long shanked hook for boat work and dapping. The body is of cinnamon herl, say from a turkey tail feather. The six legs are knotted strands of cock-pheasant centre tail. The wings are two hackle points of Cree cockerel, tied in flat, and two large ginger cock hackles are wound in for buoyancy. This is an excellent fly for bouncing about on wave-tops when fishing from a boat, but it is not suitable for the more precise and delicate attack to rising fish in a gentle ripple along the margins.

Here I need a smaller fly with a detached body. In the old days they would have used unvulcanised Indian rubber suitably stiffened with turpentine, for detached bodies. Today, if you cannot obtain the moulded plastic mayfly bodies, then a suitable body can be made by binding strands of deer hair or bucktail to a needle, sliding it off when firmly finished, and lashing it down onto the shank of the hook in the usual way. The air-chambers of the hollow hair cause the fly to be practically unsinkable.

The thought of fishing the Daddy reminds me of dapping for sea trout on Loch Maree. The area I used to fish was the furthest from the sea at Kinlochewe where Charles MacLaren used to keep his fishing hotel. Drawing a line from the roadway to a point where the great mountain of Slioch plunges down into the water, my friend and I would go across to the famous Whisky Rock, to fish along the shallow margins to the far end of the bay where the Kinlochewe river debouches into Maree.

I have never been overjoyed to use a dapping rod. It seems that I always move the fly away from the place where, an instant after, an angry boil of a frustrated sea trout misses the fly which I have just taken away. I feel more confident with the orthodox fly rod.

We made our dapping lines from a light green nylon carpet-yarn, tying in a single turn granny knot every yard or so to prevent it from teasing out. Eight yards of this material is sufficient to carry out a dapping fly in a reasonably stiff breeze.

Although I made up some bushy versions of the Daddy, with the hackle point wings tied forward to catch the wind, Maree sea trout always preferred the large black dapping-fly versions of Pennells and Zulus, dressed on size 6 and 8 fine wire low-water salmon hooks, and this is strange for there's nothing like them in nature. For buoyancy, I found it best to dress the bodies of these flies with a fine suede chenille which I smeared liberally with mucilin at the fly-tying bench. Even so, a few dunkings in the waves saturated the flies and rows of them were stuck into the boat gunwales to dry out in the wind.

It always astonished me on Maree how hooked sea trout would 'run up the line', and in dapping I would have to bat the large centre-pin reel furiously to keep in touch with the fish as it bolted under the boat, and then I would swivel rapidly round to play the fish behind the boat. Local folk-lore had it that if you were lucky enough to have a salmon roll onto the fly, then you shouldn't strike until you saw and felt the line tightening into the fish. It would happen to me, that a great salmon which had run the passage of the Ewe river into the loch, performed a classic roll onto my Daddy, and I steeled myself to respond with the equally classic pause and tighten, only nothing happened, I was left staring at the limp and lifeless blow-line.

If Maree proved either too dour or too stormy there was always the option of the small Coulin loch further up the Kinlochewe glen. At first sight it looked the most unlikely place to catch migratory fish. For all the world it resembled a Southern tench pond, until one realised that these fish had nowhere else to go except through Coulin to reach their spawning grounds. And glancing upwards to the rim of the high hills behind, sometimes I would see the silhouette of antlers of stags against the sky.

It was one night in the hotel lounge when our fishing party had all been sucking at the sauce bottle, with our fly-tying kits spread out in front, that the then landlord, Paul Jackson, himself no slouch with a fishing rod, challenged me to make a 'new' pattern of fly. Paul wasn't a dapping man but he did like to fish a large semi-dapping fly 'on the bob'.

I told him that the most renowned wet-fly for sea trout was the Teal, Blue & Silver, so I would concoct a bushy version of that. The fly was duly made, handed over and forgotten . . . until, months later I began to receive 'phone calls from Wester Ross. What, the callers demanded, were the ingredients of Paul's miracle-fly which sea trout would brutally assault from large distances, and which a legendary monster salmon had contemptuously removed from the leader with a mere flick of its massive head on Loch Coulin? I had to confess that the actual prescription was lost in the mists of time and whisky fumes, but a good approximation is included in the list of flies in the appendix.

Alas, the sea trout shoals dwindled in Maree, some say through netting at sea, some say through seals entering the loch, but my friends and I left 'for fresh woods and pastures new'.

If the wind rules in Orkney and Wester Ross, it is no minor prince in the Shetlands. I wake in the ferryboat to see Sumburgh Light sliding by the porthole in the grey light of early morning. The spindrift past the porthole tells me that the weather will be 'changeable', to repeat the euphemism of the forecast. It's not such a problem as Orkney or Maree for Shetland lochs, though numerous, are mostly small, and many of them lie in declivities between heather-covered slopes.

Shetland has more than three hundred lochs, and a hundred of them are controlled by the Shetland Fishing Association which issues an informative guide to them. The islands should be an angler's paradise, but the great sea trout shoals of yesteryear have vanished with its snows.

There's an unfair saying, 'Jack of all trades, master of none' which could describe the footloose fly-fisher, someone like myself who travels far and wide to different types of fishery in diverse places. I must be at a disadvantage to the local angler who knows his local water intimately. The obvious short-cut is to ask the local angler. This is no problem in Orkney which has a smaller number of mostly expansive lochs like Harray and Stenness. Orkney is strange in that at certain times one or two waters will be 'on' whilst others are 'off'. In Shetland, where some seventy-five miles of land surround over three hundred smaller lochs and lochans, you may be lucky to see another angler. It is 'pot luck'.

The Fishery Association in Shetland (3 Gladstone Terrace, Lerwick) publishes an informative booklet, giving details of the hundred lochs under their own control. It is accurate, showing access routes and productive fishing areas. It tells which waters are likely to hold sea trout or are to be fished mainly for brown trout. The fisher of wild places should be aware of those temptingly green patches of sphagnum, the bog moss, below which lie pits of icy water. It goes without saying that lochs in peaty areas should be waded with care, and prodding the bottom with a staff is a commonsense precaution.

The casual visiting angler will not have encountered before the fearsome Great Skua. Wandering away from the water's edge will bring about that threatening 'Hah-hah, hah-hah' warning cry, followed by the diving attack, which is terrifying, for the clacking beak of this monstrous bird is thrust inches away from one's quivering cheeks.

In such lonely places, fishing success can only be achieved by a basic, sound technique and application of the fundamental simplicities of fly-fishing. The Shetland Angler's Association guide emphasises some sensible lessons, that trout will rise around mid-day, and again in the evening. The evening, though, is that strange Northern twilight of Summer known as the 'simmer dim' which replaces the normal hours of darkness which we enjoy in Southern climes. The changeability of Shetland weather also takes visiting anglers by surprise so that one can suddenly be plunged into a thick fog when seconds before one was bathed in bright sunshine. Even close to roads, bearings can be lost without the commonsense use of a small compass.

I always return to the dark-bodied flies when fishing anywhere North of Inverness. It would be in desperation that I abandoned the Grouse & Claret as a tail fly. I have mentioned before that I darken down the body of my Grouse & Claret, and the companion Mallard & Claret, by adding a pinch of brother Mole's fur to the claret dubbing. It's strange, that although we are preoccupied with choice of fly-dressing. I cannot remember where I read about the trick of mixing two or more dubbings to gain greater killing power. Skues hit on a captivating combination of hare's ear and yellow seal's fur for the bodies of flies which require an olive effect. When wet, this mixture is remarkably translucent.

The Mallard & Claret was probably invented by William Murdoch of Aberdeen. I have always thought the grouse-winged version to be a more effective fly because of its stronger and bolder wing. This is the older pattern, one of these probably imported from Ireland a long time ago. It is said, too, that Murdoch changed to the mallard wing because he found the grouse tail feather to be too short for large sea trout and salmon flies.

It was 'Lemon Grey' in his classic book *Torridge Fishery* who first impressed on me the importance of 'style' in fly-dressing. He emphasised that a wing should be slim, the body and hackle skimpy so that the fly would be lively in the water, and not just a soggy mess. One day, when making up some Mallard & Claret flies, this Master ran out of the claret dubbing. He casually added a rump of yellow dubbing, and claimed that the resulting fly with a mixed body was a great killer. Alas, he had not invented a new fly, Irish variations have long included a version of the famous fly with a bright yellow tail.

My choice of the Grouse & Claret in Shetland waters is to give me two bites at the cherry, for not only do brown trout relish it, but it proves to be attractive to sea trout.

The birth of the famous Ke-He fly for Orkney and Shetland lochs is that the two inventors, David Kemp and Bernard Heddle, noticed that a strong breeze was carrying a mass of small dark bees onto Loch Harray. I have often wondered if the phenomenon was really a profuse fall of drone flies which hatch out from shallow water from that ugly curiosity, the rat-tailed maggot. This beast lives underwater but obtains air through a telescopic whip-lash appendage, much like the schnorkels of German U-boats in the latter days of the last war. Regular anglers on Hanningfield Reservoir, in Essex, recognise the value of having a drone fly copy in their boxes, for the West wind brings these flies down to the body of the lake from the far shallows.

The Ke-He is an easy fly to dress. The body is thickly-wound bronze peacock herl, with a golden pheasant tippet tail and a hackle of Rhode Island Red cockerel hackle. The Scottish fly-tyer, Tom Stewart claimed that there was an alternative killing pattern which substituted a black rook feather for the legs, but I think the inventors were right to stick to the stiffer cockerel hackles, for it is sensible to use stiff fibres for the legs of bob-flies on wind-swept waters. They are more lively and sparkling in the ripple. For this reason, I would prefer a bob-fly which has a palmered hackle, say the Kate MacLaren.

The Shetland Angler's Association guide intelligently advises the use of only two flies on the leader. It seems to be simplistic. I well remember when first fishing Cow Green reservoir, in the high Pennines, that I only had to brush a tuft of cotton grass on the back cast to turn the three-fly cast into a heap of knitting. For bank fishing in windy places I invariably rely on two flies, very widely spaced. They would be the ubiquitous Grouse & Claret on the point and the Kate MacLaren as a bob-fly. The options could be used, but not that tangle-free set-up. As I won a leg of the only competition I ever fished — on Lough Conn — with just two flies when other competitors were hanging out teams of four, I rarely feel at a disadvantage.

I realise that in recommending a very narrow choice of fly I have taken both pleasure and mystery out of fly-fishing. This was not my intention. It is true that when you travel far and high to the places which the wind rules, the range of insect life is narrower. Fish are still capricious, even, paradoxically, when food supply is poorer than in the fat lands of the Southern lowlands. Their moodiness is dependent on wind and weather, and those unrecognisable factors which boil down to plain dourness. Ripping flies off the leader is rarely the answer, except to restore one's own confidence. It is merely a question of persistence with patterns which have proved their worth for a century or more, until the time, place and mood of the fish all mesh together. It's that simple.

Chironomid Pupa

Chapter 8
Blagdon and After

'Blagdon, farewell! I part from thee with pain.
I love thee well, and hope to come again
In better days, when trout are on the rise,
And rainbows, too — not only in the skies.'

Blagdon, Farewell a poem by 'H.S.T.' first
publish in Blagdon Parish Magazine, July 1917

In recent years fish farmers discovered ways to grow rainbow trout to huge weights. Naturally this caused controversy. Was it fair to claim a record for a fish which had been grown artificially to a weight in excess of the existing record, then to plant it out into a small 'put-and-take' fishery and invite one or two well-known anglers to compete for its capture within hours of its introduction into the fishery? It seemed absurd to me. Although the angling establishment accepted this state of affairs, the average angler seemed to grow cynical and sceptical about the exercise.

I was amused to read that, according to one authority, these fish were 'a superstrain of trout which made better use of the existing food supply'. I asked him if he caught Billy Bunter scoffing cream buns in his larder, if that would represent a superstrain of human being making better use of the food supply?

When it came down to it, we were simply being treated to the ordinary rainbow trout which was being fattened-up in the stew ponds by intensive feeding techniques. Later, we were also treated to cross strains of trout, Tiger Trout and so on, which were all to appear in the record fish lists. I began to reflect on the discredited theories of the late lamented academician T. D. Lysenko, who, when Minister of Agriculture of the Soviet Union, declared that genetic theory was bunkum because characteristics acquired by an organism in its own lifetime could be transmitted to the next generation. One would only have to paint black spots onto a chub to produce subsequently a race of trout.

It soon became clear that, far from these fattened fish making better use of the existing food supply, if they were not caught fairly quickly after their introduction into small fisheries, then their weight and condition rapidly deteriorated, so much so that when, later, covered in fungus, they had to be netted out of water and destroyed.

It's plain common sense that there is a relationship between food supply and the number of mouths to be fed. If you take Blagdon, the annual catches recorded in the early years of this century would create an outcry today if spread over a single month. From a food-supply point of view, present day stocking to meet fishing demand can rarely be met by the natural food in many fisheries, though fortunately the rod pressure relieves the demand before it becomes a problem.

The fishery manager at Blagdon, the famous Donald Carr, first introduced rainbow trout into the reservoir in 1905. Their average size was from 4–6". Compare this to the size of fish stocked into still-water today! These small fish were put into Blagdon in May of that year, and by August of the same year they were averaging up to 2lb in weight. In 1906 there was a widescale death of the stickleback population in Blagdon resulting in the fall-off in condition of the rainbow trout, so no further stocking of the species was undertaken for three years, though Donald Carr claimed that rainbows were spawning in his feeder streams and repopulating the lake.

By the end of the Great War, when Blagdon had settled down, fish of between 5 and 7lb were being taken in reasonable numbers by the good anglers. Thus a correspondent in the *Fishing Gazette* claimed to have caught thirteen fish between 5lb and 6½lb between 1906 and 1919. This sportsman returned all fish of under 2lb, and during those years intervening he killed 549 trout weighing 1,337lb. Though creditable, this catch would be unremarkable on many fisheries of today. Against an annual total catch of 818 fish in the year 1918, and 1,054 in 1919, it is a considerable achievement. The lighter stocking policy and the lower rod pressure would mean that the lake in those days was virtually a 'wild fish' water.

Compare this to the scene which met my eyes one day at Draycote, which my friend, Colin North and I labelled the 'Wild West Show'. The restocking tank was towed around the perimeter track by a Land-Rover, behind which followed a convoy of private cars bristling with rods. As the tank stopped at restocking places, and the wardens carried stockfish down to the water in nets, so did an army of rodded-up anglers scurry down to the water's edge. Freshly stocked fish have a habit of breaking water, presumably to gain additional oxygen after the confines of the tank, giving the false impression of rising. Each whorl was bombarded by dozens of lures, making the surface of the water look like a miniature battle of Jutland. Then the convoy would hurry away to the next stocking place.

I count myself lucky to have fished Blagdon when the relationship between stockfish and rod pressure was reasonable enough to endow the fishing with some romance from the past. It was still the Mecca which Bernard Venables graphically described in his *Angler's Testament*. It had still that captivating combination of being dour for hours on end, and then the explosive climax of a heavy fish taking the fly. The great road bridge to Wales had not then been built. If one was on the bank at sun-up one might well have the entire lake to oneself until breakfast time. 'Limititis' and competition fever had not yet invaded the land.

I was lucky enough to fish Blagdon at a time when there was a strong current of opinion running against still-water fly-fishing. The angling press was either disinterested, or downright opposed to it, and the chief prophet of coarse fishing, Richard Walker, castigated Tom Ivens in the *Angling Times*, describing the long-casting techniques from the banks of reservoirs as 'boneheaded athleticism'. Later he did a *volte-face*, and this tergiversation was caused by the opening of Grafham on his doorstep. The unfashionable branch of fly-fishing brought about uncrowded banks, but until the early sixties, there was also a lack of evolution in fly patterns and techniques.

At Blagdon, this manifested itself in two ways. In the rustic fishing hut the glass-cased denizens of yesteryear were accompanied, more often than not, by the monstrous salmon flies on which they had been caught; Jock Scotts and Dusty Millers for example. Only the most rudimentary attempts had been made to simulate the natural flies which caused the famed 'Blagdon boil' of an evening. It was not uncommon to meet anglers who were frustrated to the point of tears on having numerous swirls in front of them, with great nebs and dorsals breaking the surface, whilst the lures would be dragged through the area of activity without eliciting the slightest interest.

Only occasionally would any intellectual attempt be made to fathom out the cause of the 'boil' and then it was usually wide of the mark. Some said it was the Brown Silverhorn sedge which was the target, the fly known locally as the Grouse Tail. Others opined it was the minute *Caenis*, the Angler's Curse, which was too small to copy. More often than not the rise was to the ubiquitous *Chironomid* pupa, the buzzer, and because the hatching insect was usually taken just below the surface, the cause was unnoticed. And because the Silverhorns and *Caenis* were often hatching at the same time, and visible because they were being ignored by the fish in preference to the more vulnerable buzzer, then the wrong conclusions were reached.

It was not difficult for my friend and me to detect the cause of the Blagdon boil. Simply spooning fish revealed masses of packed buzzer pupae in their stomachs. Consultation with Blagdon regulars revealed that there was a local nymph pattern to copy the green pupa, and these we tied up, only to find them practically useless. The body of the fly was of smooth silk, ribbed with flat tinsel, and the head was of bronze peacock herl. There was no attempt to copy the marked, segmented effect of the natural pupa, nor to simulate its hooked abdomen. We photographed and enlarged samples of the pupae in order to produce an accurate copy, and we studied the way in which Blagdon trout harvested these creatures of a summer's evening.

A common buzzer pupa at Blagdon had a body of prominent black and white segments, and this was copied by winding onto a hook shank, side by side, strands of black and white horsehair. The thorax was a dubbing of mole's fur topped off with a turn or two of bronze peacock herl for the head. I deliberately made no attempt at that time to add materials for the tail appendages and breathing tubes because the fly was designed to pierce the surface film quickly when the water was mostly calm and 'sticky', and it was to be targetted accurately at individual fish taking the natural pupae just below the surface film. This method resulted from my dry-fly upbringing. It was the year in which Newcastle won the cup, and with that team's distinctive black and white striped shirts, the name of 'Footballer' entered the lists of successful fly patterns, where it has been ever since, and for one period of time, it held the record-fish capture at Grafham.

In recent years I have updated the Footballer, giving it tail and head fibres of fine, fluorescent white floss. It also became difficult for me to find really good horsehair, and I reverted to Lunn's old trick of making fly-bodies of stripped cock hackle stalks, the black and white ones being wound side by side from half-way round the hook bend to make a perfectly tapered body. It was necessary to change the thorax-dubbing, to a light chestnut colour, for, strangely enough, no matter what colour the natural pupa has, the thoraces are invariably of a light brown. I think my earlier mistake in colour was through using as a model pupae which had been spooned out of fishy stomachs, and these were partially bleached by the action of digestive juices.

Identifying different colours of buzzer pupae in different waters, I varied body colours of the Footballer. Blagdon produced a fawny version, also a greeny-olive. The large black 'racehorses' emerged at Chew Valley and Darwell had its scarlet one. Two Lakes was the home to the genuine black-and-white original, as was Hanningfield. I claim that the Footballer was the very first accurate copy of the buzzer pupa. It still works to this day, even though subsequent innovators have produced many other copies.

A floating version was produced simply by adding a badger hackle and a pair of glassy-white hackle point wings, sloping backwards. The dry version was only partially successful, sometimes later in the hatch when females were returning to the water to lay eggs. The trouble is that the buzzer hatch is usually so prolific that trout have no trouble cruising at a leisurely pace through myriads of pupae trapped in the surface film, cropping them en-route. The dry-fly unhappily appealed only to smaller fish which took them in a splashy rise.

The very first day in which my companion and I attacked the Blagdon boil with the Footballer was quite remarkable, a satisfying example of 'oneupmanship'. Along the bank of Butcombe Bay the usual frustration was taking place, furious casting by neighbours with swearing and curses, mutterings about 'bloody *Caenis*', and so on. I took four superb fish in almost as many casts, and an unsolicited letter later appeared in the columns of *Trout & Salmon* magazine to comment on this. Many years later, the Footballer hoisted me with my own petard, when returning fishless from a prolific rise at Hanningfield, I tied up to a boat from which the angler was lifting a limit catch of splendid fish . . . . 'On your Footballer', he smugly announced. And I had mistakenly assumed the fish were taking sedge and had fruitlessly fished through the rise with Invictas!

Omissions and mistakes, we all make them, and I never hit on the strategy of making and fishing a hatching buzzer, nor thought of it until the suspender versions were invented by someone else, using a tiny ball of polystyrene as a floatation device. It would have been simple enough to have clipped short a badger cock hackle to make a Footballer bog down in the surface film. I realise now that I never thought of this simply because the technique of Footballer fishing was to cast quickly and accurately at a visible target, pushing the fly through the surface film in front of its nose.

'Blagdon was a regular pilgrimage'.

Blagdon was a regular pilgrimage, staying with my old friends, the Gullivers, who kept the pleasant *Live & Let Live* pub in the village. Anglers remark that they have missed fish along the Butcombe Bank when they have been seduced by the sight of the sun falling behind the hills, the lights twinkling from cottage windows as a deathly calm falls across the lake, and, far out, the monstrous fish send ripples flowing outwards as they break surface to take a fly.

The last few casts I made at Blagdon, as the first shades of night began to fall, were with the Hoolet moth, and I aimed at the large fish patrolling the shadows, under the pines, in search of the succulent moths which blundered into the water and couldn't escape. Their struggles could be copied by heaving out this giant floating fly, then tugging it back in short hauls of line. A heart-stopping moment was when a huge rainbow bow-waved after the fly, like a Jack Russell spelling out doom to a fleeing rat. If, in anxiety, you slowed the fly, the fish turned away, but, if by keeping your nerve, you attempted escape, a furious whorl and tug was usually the reward.

The Hoolet, that age-old pattern, is the perfect moth copy. The fuzzy peacock herl was wound over a sliver of cork. The wing, tied flat, was from a brown owl's wing in those days. You would have to find some other feather today, the bird rightly being protected. The poet tells us of the silent flight of the owl, and its wing-strokes are muffled by a myriad of tiny hairs on the feathers. These filaments gave floatability to the bulky Hoolet fly, and to all of those Bustard flies which used to employ the same feather and delight the night angler for sea trout on Border streams.

The late-coming of genuinely imitative flies to Blagdon was because the water rightly had the reputation of being a 'stickleback' paradise. Often I would see trout beating up the weed-beds to drive the tiddlers into open water where they could be trapped against the surface. This explains the frankly provocative lures over decades of use, and the invention of the Jersey Herd, probably by Cyril Inwood, though accredited to Tom Ivens, was a boon. It kills well to this day and has outlived the once-popular polystickle.

I dressed a black and silver version of the Jersey Herd. I likewise substituted a glittering gold tinsel for the quieter one which was originally the coppery metal, cut in strips, from the top of a Jersey Herd milk bottle, from which the lure derived its name. I soon learned at Blagdon, and later at Chew, that two types of lure were needed to catch the trout when they were on a sticklebacking beat. In bright sunlight a shining lure like the Jersey Herd reflected the sun's rays. Fry and sticklebacks were transformed into drab camouflage-coated survivors when the sky was sombre, and Ivens' Green and Brown nymph was practicularly effective.

There has been a classical controversy in still-water fly-fishing about the provocative lure as against insect-imitating flies and nymphs. I regard it as unimportant, since if one is attacking a 'sticklebacker' with a fry imitation, then that is fishing imitatively on the food which the fish is taking. It was at Hanningfield, the big Essex reservoir near to Chelmsford, that this was brought home to me. When the lake first opened for fly-fishing there were glorious surface rises because numerous shoals of perch were gleaning the weed-beds and silty areas of the bottom. I think it was Darwin who pointed out that two separate species cannot thrive together if they feed in the same way in the same habitat. Then perch dominated the deep water; the trout came to the surface.

The perch were decimated by a disease and the rich larder near to the bottom of the lake was then opened to the trout. The activity on the surface declined, for every time a patch of weed was brought up on the anchor, boat anglers would see that it was stuffed full of small fish and insects of every kind. It was plain commonsense to fish with sunken line and lures. This was when my 'Beastie'-type lures were invented.

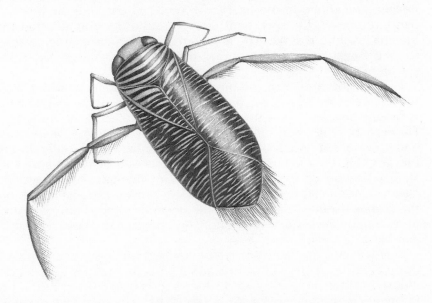

Corixa (water boatman)

The idea came to me when I was fishing with a friend, Dr Tony Richards. To work his flies more deeply, Tony pinched a lead shot onto the head of a marabou lure. Immediately he began to latch on to powerful rainbows. As he retrieved his weighted lure I noticed that it worked in an entirely different way to the unweighted one that I was using. Firstly, between retrieves, the lure darted downwards, nose first, but the weighted head caused the long marabou tail to flutter and vibrate in a fascinating way.

I decided to sophisticate this at the fly-tying bench. Firstly, I lapped a long shank hook with black floss, and ribbed it with silver tinsel. Then I tied in a bouquet of bright orange marabou feathers as a throat hackle. Two wings were next tied in, but on either side of the hook shank, and these were the tips of marabou feathers which extended well beyond the hook bend. Outside of these were two cheeks of barred silver pheasant flank feathers, much in the American streamer style. Finally, two layers of lead wire were lashed around the head of the fly and varnished black. The first time the Beastie was cast in anger upon the waters of Hanningfield, it settled like a feather duster upon the surface until the fast-sinking line submerged it. My companion, horror-struck, remarked: 'I've heard of hen-feathers but this is the first time I've seen someone use the whole bloody chicken!' Shortly afterwards a fish hit the fly like an express. It was common to find the entire Beastie embedded in the back of a trout's throat, and the hooked fish tore line off the reel, bent the rod into a hoop and bolted for the shallow bird reserve. The line literally hissed through the water, for the Beastie seemed to bring out a predatory ferocity in its pursuer.

It was a forerunner of the more popular Dognobbler, which also used a weighted head and marabou plume, but I think the Beastie is more versatile in its action, even though it takes longer to make. Fluorescent white and pink, lime and orange, versions were used and duly named 'Voodoo' lures. A big advantage of these lures was the fact that they would float for just a second or two before the sinking line pulled them under. One of my favourite tactics was to cast to a surface-feeding fish which would make a diving attack on the lure as it sank. This gave me the uncanny opportunity of saying to a companion, as if clairvoyant, 'I will get a take about now . . .' and bang, the fish would be on.

This was not the first time I had adapted the ideas of friends. A dour evening at Bewl Water caused me to remark that I had enjoyed better days. My friend, Bill Roberts replied that he had a fail-never nymph in his box. I said 'That's good news,' which baptised the fly the 'Good News Nymph'. I was astonished when he passed it over, for it was nothing more than a parcel of fuzzy dubbing around a long shanked hook. The secret lay in the mixture of dubbings, four colours, and the rear-half of the hook only had been lapped with lead wire before this mixture was applied. The second cast attracted a fish, and I progressed to an evening limit. On reflection, it made sense, for this was a summer's evening, sedge were hatching, and this fly imitated, both in size and colour, the sedge pupa rising to the surface to hatch. The subtle weighting balanced it in the water exactly to match the swimming behaviour of the caddis grub. The deadly dubbing mixture on that occasion was of orange, olive, yellow seal's fur with a few strands of blue, the overall effect being a glowing amber. The successful retrieve which attracted the fish was a series of long, steady hauls.

Whether to fish from the bank or go afloat is hardly a controversy. Tom Ivens chose to fish from the bank in post-war years because it was cheaper. I have a slight preference for bank fishing because I have more scope for working out tactical ideas. When the Suspender Nymph was born, to copy the moment of hatching of the buzzer pupa into the adult fly, I wasn't happy with the polystyrene ball, thinking it too bulky and inert. I considered that a collar of stiff fibres would give better effect. It struck me that if I could find a fine deer hair, that very tiny muddlers would do the trick.

By simplifying the muddler dressing into a thin body and ribbing, followed by the ruffe of closely cropped hair, the 'Skinhead' hatching nymph was created in various colours, black, olive, red. They enjoyed a memorable night when the wind was sweeping waves along the dam wall at Hanningfield. All that was needed was to cast a team of three of these flies upwind with floating line and greased leader, then to allow them to drift round, curving the leader to give a modest drag. The fish hit them with enthusiasm, the black and greeny-olive bodied flies being the most successful.

The strangest, perhaps the most difficult question to answer in still-water fly-fishing is what fly to use when there are no indications of fly choice, no surface rise, no insects in the air, no swifts diving on the water, no small food-fish along the margins . . . nothing. This tests confidence in a 'general fly'. In salmon fishing, no problem, on goes the Willie Gunn. On a trout reservoir, when I'm in doubt, then I usually tie on a team of three variants of Richard Walker's famous Sweeny Todd. Mine are dressed on normal wet-fly hooks, sizes 8 and 10, and the fluorescent thoraces and matching hackles are green, yellow or orange instead of the shocking pink which the Old Master decreed. We call these flies Sweeny Variant Mini-lures.

Thus it was that, coming off Bewl Water with a catch which totalled 7.5lb, I asked my young son, Simon, who had been fishing with me, to book in my catch whilst I waited for him in the car. I was startled to read in the angling press the following week that a junior angler had caught a monster 7½lb fish at Bewl . . . seems he had forgotten to write in my name and the number of fish which made up that weight! The fish had fallen victim to the min-Sweenies.

Blagdon did bring home the problem of the Brown Silverhorn, for unlike Chew, the more popular Cinnamon Sedge was relatively scarce. Both brown and black Silverhorns were prolific at Blagdon, though the black version was never taken. The brown one would be accepted by trout when buzzers and lake olives weren't hatching, so a copy of the fly was necessary. I only used the Silverhorn as a dry-fly at Blagdon, and the distinctively striped black and white horns were copied by tying in two stripped grizzle cock hackles. These stalks also carry the 'bullseye' effect of the whole feather.

The body was fashioned simply from dark olive tying silk. The two hackles, throat and body were of furnace cock, the body feather being ribbed with fine gold wire. The wing was taken from the grouse tail feather, and tied flat, as a rolled wing. It's a curiosity that, although nearly all still-water sedges can be copied by the standard cinnamon sedge pattern, brown Silverhorns are distinctive enough to require an individual usurper, as Richard Walker discovered when motivated to invent his own Longhorn flies.

I was witnessing the weigh-in of match anglers on Lough Conn when I noticed that one trout being held by its captor had an unusual orange belly. The angler explained to me that this was a rare Gillaroo type of fish which dined almost entirely on snail, which gave it that colouration. He invited me to press its stomach whereon I felt a crunchy sensation and its gaping mouth promptly disgorged a stream of black shells which must have reduced its weight considerably. These Gillaroos sometimes desert their grovelling habit to come up for the odd mayfly, which is how this one fell victim in the competition. Compared to the normal brown trout in Conn, they fight poorly.

It has been recorded over many years that about ten percent of Blagdon fish become specialist corixa-feeders. They develop thicker walls to their stomachs to cope with the hard shells. Some anglers believe that only alkaline waters contain sufficient calcium for the shells of the water-boatman, but this is not so; one species does grow and thrive in acidic waters, (Scotti) so it is worthwhile fishing the corixa even in peaty waters.

Yet corixa fishing is not easy, it's a question of fishing 'blind'. I recollect fishing a bay at Bough Beach reservoir with John Goddard who was a regular rod there at that time and familiar with the water. He told me that fish would enter the bay at roughly four in the afternoon to search for corixa until the evening rise to buzzer and sedge would begin. Changing his fly to suit the corixa tactic he was soon into a fish. Are there migrations of corixa from one area to another? Worthington and Macan tell us in their book *Life in Lakes and Rivers* that corixa are preyed on extensively by fish when they move onto an unaccustomed background which doesn't match their behaviour pattern and colouration. When first attempting to come to grips with the Blagdon corixa-feeders, I looked up some fourteen species of the little beasts, but, happily, all of them could be copied with a single artificial.

I used to fish the corixa as a single fly on a very long leader into bays like Butcombe, using a floating line and allowing the weighted fly to sink to the bottom. The activity of the corixa is to move in short, jerky darts, often towards the surface to collect a little store of air to tuck under its tummy. This is an easy behaviour pattern to copy in retrieving the line, for corixa fishing, though slow and patient, is simple and rewarding. It may be pure coincidence, but I discovered, too, that Blagdon fish seemed to move into the bays in later afternoon to hunt down the paddling creatures.

The fly is easy to make by winding white floss over a lead wire base, ribbing it with brown button-thread. A silver tinsel tag can be tied in to copy the air bubble. The back is a strip of feather from tail to head, varnished to give the shiny shell-like effect. The extended fibres are separated on either side of the head with figure-of-eight windings to make the paddles. Although Ireland boasts its Gillaroo and Sonaghan specialised-feeding trout, the Blagdon corixa-eating brownies are the only example of similar adaption I have encountered in mainland lakes. Even waters which are prolific in snails which trout feed upon, do not produce an equivalent race of Gillaroos.

Corixidae are a useful barometer of the balance between fish stocks, food supply and rod pressure. The simple commercial pressure to stock fish at a level to satisfy increased demand for fishing soon denudes the shallows of species like the water boatman. This is when fish caught several days after introduction are found to be empty of food. This is when you wade into the water and see no small creatures scampering away from the commotion you are causing. Perhaps the rod pressure must be satisfied, and bills have to be paid. There can be remedies; sanctuary areas for wildlife where insect life is regenerated, or even places where fly-boards and tile-kilns encourage the flies, bugs and so on to replenish their species. Otherwise we shall breed ourselves a race of anglers who are content to bombard uneducated rainbow trout with dognobblers, the put-and-take extreme.

Chapter 9
Two Lakes and Innocence

'The ceremony of innocence is drowned.'

The Turn of the Screw Benjamin Britten

My excuses for innocence are that, firstly, I was reared on wild brown trout in our isolated stream the former Kent River Board used to stock, but only with fingerling trout. When I graduated to Weirwood reservoir in 1958, experience of stocking lakes with rainbow trout was limited, perhaps due to the policy of Donald Carr at Blagdon who also stocked with smaller fish in the prewar years. I was, when young, interested in the fish and the fishing. Fishery policy I took for granted, believing the trout in all waters to be relatively wild.

The legend of Alex Behrendt at Two Lakes is well-known. He was a prisoner of war in this country though with a peacetime experience of fishery management. After the war he stayed here and bought a parcel of land between the Rivers Test and Itchen. He scooped out six lakes of various sizes, depths and shapes which were fed from a stream.

Alex Behrendt was aware of the problem of put-and-take fishing whereby 'tame' pellet-fed fish might be caught within hours of being planted out into the fishery. Unlike many commercial fisheries which have sprung up since, he used various techniques to give an element of 'wildness' to his trout. For example, fish were taken from his feeding pens some days before their release and transferred to a cage in one of the large lakes. During the acclimatisation period they were not fed artificially and so they were compelled to hunt for their natural food within the limits of the cage. Then, one day the cage would be removed and the 'free-range fish' would disperse into the body of the lake. To encourage surface feeding the fish which were being reared in the pens were fed on floating pellets which had to be taken from the surface.

One lake, the 'Home Pool', was reserved only for fish which had been introduced at the fingerling stage. They became very wary indeed, and those anglers who rightly prided themselves as skilled fishermen, Barry Welham, David Jacques, Oliver Kite, tested themselves against these worthy opponents. On the 'Home Pool' it was important to fish with copies of the insect life of the fishery.

Alex Behrendt had been told that the acid soil of this New Forest land would not be conducive to fly life, but his own instincts were proved right by the wide variety of insects which the lakes produced. It was at this time that the knowledgeable entomologist and angler, C. F. Walker published his standard textbook, *Lake Flies and their Imitation*, introducing many of us to such delights as the Sepia and Claret Duns. Many of the examples of these still-water flies came from Two Lakes.

It is fashionable to criticise put-and-take still-water fisheries, and I, too, am critical of excessive 'knock 'em down and drag 'em out' as Two-Ton Tony Galento used to say. I have always respected Alex Behrendt for the trouble he used to take to ensure that his fish responded to imitative fly-fishing. An advantage which smaller lakes have over the big reservoirs is in their wider variety of fly life. The Sepia Dun is a case in point. In April it would be welcomed in much the same way at Two Lakes as mayflies on the Test. The Sepia Dun also took me by surprise in my first season there, for I was astonished by the arrival of the myriads of the dark brown duns on the surface. The fish hit them enthusiastically, not looking at anything else, and I had no copy in my box. I expressed my frustration to Ollie Kite, who promptly opened a well stocked fly box and selected a C. F. Walker copy from the serried ranks of flies.

'I thought you only carried half-a-dozen patterns?' I said.

'Ah, don't believe everything you read,' he replied, eyes twinkling. And Ollie's fly did the trick.

The Sepia Dun was welcomed by me because it was a fly which trout would unhesitatingly take from the surface. The dry-fly was easy to make from a dark-brown herled body with gold rib and matching hackle and tail fibres. Alex encouraged dry-fly fishing, reserving one of his lakes for that technique.

This was a long pool with thick bushes along the far bank. It was one of the rare homes of the electric-blue damsel fly where the trout would leap high into the air to catch the adult fly which had that deadly habit of hovering stationary a foot or so above the water. Even C. F. Walker hadn't prescribed medicine for the adult damsel. I wrote to John Veniard for some bright blue lurex, which, with a black button-thread ribbing, made a perfect body for the damsel when lapped along a mayfly hook. Two grey partridge hackles were splayed out in the spent-gnat position for the wings, then a badger cock hackle and black ostrich herl head finished the dry artificial. It dealt out death to many great trout at Two Lakes.

The problem at Two Lakes was the sheer variety of fly life, hence Ollie Kite's well stuffed fly box. The pond and lake olives were no problem, the dear old Greenwell served for both of those, but I met with preoccupied feeding on the spent spinners for the first time, and until Oliver Kite introduced me to his Apricot Spinner, I pressed the Lunn's Particular into service. The late David Jacques specialised in fishing the sedge, invariably as a floater. I asked him how many species there were at Two Lakes. He mentioned some astronomical number, and his crowded fly box revealed that he made distinct copies of all of them. I was joined one evening by John Goddard, the recognised authority on anglers' flies, and he was so entranced by the rich choice of insect life that he spent so much time bug-hunting with his net that huge slurping trout passed him by, unnoticed.

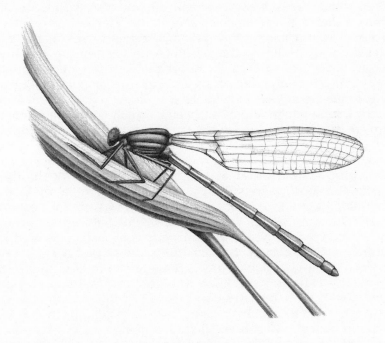

Damsel fly

Of course, before long the Two Lakes enterprise was bound to be copied. Commercial trout fisheries sprang up all over the country. At first the managers also adopted techniques to bring a true wildness and free-range feeding habit into the fisheries. This was true at Coldingham Loch, high on the cliffs near to St Abb's Head and the navigator's 'measured mile'. It was an eery experience to see the Great Red Sedge doing its whirling-dervish dance out on the loch whilst the lonely cries of sea-birds echoed in my ears from the cliffs behind. This was an old Irish lough fly, the Murrough. The Irish dress it with a green body, but I found a dark claret dubbing more to the taste of Scottish fish, palmered with a dark red hackle and winged with speckled hen feather.

The big mystery to those of us who were working out imitative flies and techniques for the early smaller still-water fly-fisheries was the Phantom Larva. It is virtually transparent, yet on so many occasions did I find a gelatinous mess in the stomachs of Two Lakes' trout, that I knew they were not 'invisible men' to the fish. John Goddard told me that he thought it impossible to copy the Phantom. I thought that the jelly-baby did have the faintest turquoise colour, and I know that David Collyer tried wrapping clear polythene around a silver-shanked hook. More successful was Richard Walker's Barny Google, also made from a body of clear polythene with a prominent pair of red-bead eyes at the top. Successful was the Barny Google, but as a copy of the spectrous Phantom larva, who can say? I never pursued this quest further, though I had the intention to try to find a clear plastic with the slightest blue-green haze in its make-up.

There was a golden age of still-water fishing when management adopted techniques to relate the behaviour of the fish to the natural environment. It was inevitable that this would change. Rod pressure naturally increased, and with it came match fishing with its relaxation of bag-limits. The virus of 'limititis' pervaded the sport where so many anglers believed that the permit price entitled them to a limit bag, and if this was not forthcoming, then the stocking policy was at fault. A laughable extreme was when an ignorant party of Southern reservoir anglers berated the landlord of a hotel with fishing rights on Loch Maree for not restocking the water. Managements were forced to concede to this pressure by shooting stockfish straight from stew ponds into fisheries, with no acclimatisation period. To their credit, the two fisheries I first visited, Two Lakes and Coldingham, to this day maintain a policy to encourage natural feeding by the fish. For the extreme put-and-take fisheries, though, you might as well use an April Fool's joke I once made, a trout pellet glued to a hook shank with a hackle in front. On being questioned by a curious watcher, I confirmed:

'Ah, that's my edible trout fly.'

Absurdities began to creep into still-water fly-fishing; at one extreme the 'Northampton Sandwich' whereby the perpetrator takes a mouthful of bread and then chokes into a fit of coughing which sprays crumbs onto the water. I heard of an ingenious cigarette holder which doubled up as a blow-pipe for trout pellets. In competition there was the trick of breaking the spine of a slightly undersized fish, then stretching it to the size limit. The coarse-fisherman's floating 'caster' was much in demand. It came down to a new psychology, that many anglers thought they were paying for a limit-bag of trout rather than the privilege to fish in pleasant countryside.

Inevitably this rubbed off on the managements of the small fisheries which were competing for custom with the large reservoirs. They had to cater for this mood with more and bigger fish, and the voracious rainbow trout soon cleared entire species of insect life from these fisheries so that the art of fly-dressing and imitative fly-fishing became superfluous. Happily, the pendulum is swinging the other way. Some fisheries introduce size limits for the fly, and where they have numerous lakes, they are allocated to different techniques. Hence at Lakedown there is a dry-fly only pool, another for dry-fly and nymph and yet a third for floating line only. Perhaps the excess of what the Americans call 'dude fisheries' has passed. Richard Walker was joking when he invented his 'Fagendus Fly'. Or was he?

A problem was that the ingenious C. F. Walker took 'perfect imitation' to the extreme that when photographed side by side for the colour plates of his book, in a swift glance it was hard to tell which was the natural and which the artificial fly. Taking one pattern at random, the Hoglouse, I simplified his pattern to a grey rabbit's fur body, ribbed with oval silver tinsel and a grey partridge hackle wound around the hook bend to give the impression of the creature's legs trailing out behind. It did enjoy some success, but although we spoon the stomachs of trout from various waters, as far as I know there's been no systematic analysis of the proportions of insects and bugs which trout accept in smaller fisheries. True, I did find the odd hoglouse in stomach contents, but being an easy target, slow moving and prolific in many ponds, I would have expected gorging on this beast on occasion, as you find, for example, with snail migrations. It was not the case.

C. F. Walker was a prophet before his time in imitating the damsel larva. For many years anglers ignored his insistence on the usefulness and importance of this creature. I first noticed that anglers were making copies of the large olive variety at Bewl Water, and before long it was being swum through most fisheries for most of the year. Against this experience though is the curious fact that some beasts which would appear to be vulnerable are rarely, if ever taken. The Pond Skater is a case in point, and although I have been told they are on occasion acceptable, I have never found the Great Diving Beetle (*Dytiscus marginalis*) inside a trout, and I expect its formidable jaws are a deterrent.

What is surprising is the extent to which stock-fish, especially rainbows, will 'hoover-up' the insect stock of a fishery. When I was managing the Sundridge Lake fisheries in Kent and before we chose to introduce trout, I asked John Goddard to undertake an insect survey of the fishery. In passing, I apologise for using this term 'insect' as a convenient term in a loose way. It's true that a boffin can pick me up if I call a true bug an insect, but at a practical angling level, we must use an understandable vocabulary which is why we call all sorts of larvae and pupae 'nymphs' when, plainly they are not, and this culminates in the absurdity of the 'Jersey Herd' nymph for that famous stickleback imitation. Before the trout were introduced into the lakes, the shallows were swarming with water-boatmen. It was noticeable that within a few weeks of the fish being put into the lake, these sandy banks were swept clean.

What we disparagingly dub as 'put-and-take' fisheries had to happen to meet the growing demand for fly-fishing, especially in areas where true stream fishing is scarce. In its first growth period of intensive competition some fisheries relied on big fish to be caught quickly as a way of attracting customers. Fortunately, this has changed and managements try to make the fishing more challenging by restricting hook size, and by adopting some of the ideas which Alex Behrendt pioneered at Two Lakes. Some fisheries even adopt old chalk-stream techniques to counter the voracious appetite of the rainbow trout, using fly-boards and tile-kiln farms for snails and bugs. Alex described his experiences of small-fishery management in his book *The Management of Angling Waters*. Fisheries were overcoming the misfortune of their anglers reporting that the trout they caught were completely empty, and reverting to the experience of Mr Sinclair-Cunningham who, during the early days at Coldingham, emptied the stomach of a huge rainbow of a gourmet's delight of small fish, frog spawn and a pint or so of weed.

In the last century, that renowned keeper of the Houghton water on the Test, W. J. Lunn, introduced the fly-board. His techniques of 'mixing the blood' of fly-stocks, and renewing the food-cycles of his fisheries were as important as caring for the more obvious and visible fish stocks. It is true that a small lake fishery could exist with virtually no fly life, the fish would go in and come out again within a short time of their introduction. The trouble is that as the greater part of fly-fishing is now done on still-water, we should lose that fascinating craft of imitative fly-dressing. Happily, there has been a sea-change in fishery-management, and, hopefully, this is being reflected in a changing attitude by many anglers.

'. . . their dusky dark brown cousins in nearby Calder loch'.

Although I was captivated by a small lake fishery at Shepbear, in Devon, with its carefully acclimatised stock of Loch Leven brown trout, I was never going to remain wedded to the small fisheries. This lake was all that I wanted in a small fishery. It was lightly fished and the trout had become rusé. On a sunny afternoon the village lads would have a swimming party, and I would wander round the small, medieval church by the lakeside where the ancient knight-patrons lay side-by-side with their wives, fierce-looking hunting dogs at their feet and fearsome swords clutched between their mail-gauntletted hands. The evening light would bedabble the mahogany-dark wood of the pews with splotches of blue and scarlet from the windows, and the lads would whoop-it away up the lane, leaving the lake in peace and the ancient warriors to their slumbers.

Then, as the shadows lengthened, the Levens would cruise the dark shadows under the trees, sucking down the odd sedge or moth, and I would lengthen out my line to intercept them. This is how small-lake fishing should be, wild brown trout in a water which is left fallow for long periods, and even the swimming boys, with their furious splashing and frenzied shouts, served to inculcate a wariness into the fish. Yes, that is how it should be, but, alas, the economics of most fisheries render such a policy as impossible.

And those Leven trout, the bright silver fighters, were the attraction to anglers before the rainbow fever infected us. It was the fish which every owner advertised in his fishery, and it was the distinctive strain, just as the brown trout in Loch Watten are a mint-silver in comparison to their dusky dark-brown cousins in nearby Calder Loch. It was not just imagination, the Leven trout did fight harder, you could not count them beaten 'till they slid over the net's rim.

Alas, as I wearied of the smaller fisheries, my innocence waned. I was left with a fond memory of floating a white moth on the surface of the dry-fly pool at Two Lakes. The calm surface and the warm evening sun induced a soporific mood. Then the water exploded, a great trout catapulted itself into the air, and, diving down onto my fly like a Stuka, it snapped my leader as if it were cotton, leaving me to stare speechlessly at the curly end of my ruptured leader. The ripples wandered out to the lake's margin, the widening waves of regret.

The commercial success of small still-water fisheries in this country soon attracted the interest of entrepeneurs in France. I was invited to give demonstrations of casting and fishing methods at the opening of the first such fishery at Dreux, in France. In front of a sizeable gallery I moved into a double-haul routine, and succeeded in dropping a Montana nymph in front of a cruising fish.

On striking I found myself fighting a heavy fish which bore away from the bank with powerful propeller-sweeps of its broad tail. It was my first experience with the Kamloops strain of rainbow which the French favour. It has a long, streamlined body-shape with wide, sweeping caudal fins as a contrast to the corpulent Shasta strain which was popular at that time with our own fishery management. The fish eventually relented to the gasps of relief from the gallery. It pulled down the spring balance to 5.5 kilos, my best still-water trout at that time.

The stocking of large rainbows became wide-spread in our put-and-take type fisheries. It satisfied a rising demand and interest, but I was becoming disenchanted with this type of fishing. I had lost my innocence. There's a mystery about a large lake or wild river, and the sense of the unknown is an essential ingredient of my own pleasure. The challenge to future management is surely how to move on, past the present provision of material returns for ticket money, to try to bring back an element of wildness into stocked waters. It will be difficult because it implies the education of the angling public. It is curious that at Cow Green, in Teesdale, the unstocked lake where wild brown trout only abound, is lightly fished by connoisseurs, whereas the stocked rainbow reservoirs lower down the valley, at Hury and Grassholme, will be almost shoulder-to-shoulder fishing. As La Rochefoucauld sadly observed: 'Alas for human nature. Especially other peoples'.'

Chapter 10
When Seven Stars Shine

> 'Memory, through the spectacles of imagination, is a river in which the fish are always in season, always obliging; where the winds do not blow too coldly and the cast, which in the world of reality ends with a resounding splash in a horrid coil, sails through the air to land like thistledown and comes round with the precision of one of those diagrams in the books of our masters.'
>
> *Fish, Fowl and Foreign Lands* J. D. Greenway

When an expert angling writer describes his own water it is a mistake to believe that his work has limited application. Nowhere is this more true than in 'Lemon Grey's' masterpiece, *Torridge Fishery*. This author ran a fishery on the Torridge, based on his guest house, 'Devon Lodge'. He was an eccentric man who could sometimes become irascible. I was told once that a colonel who he was showing over his fishery, carelessly threw a cigarette packet down on the river bank, whereupon he exploded:

'You damn litter lout! Pack your bags and clear off home!'

And he recounts in his own book that if a hen-pecked husband arrived with a domineering battleaxe wife, he would invite the lady to leave and the husband to stay to enjoy his fishing. It was this writer who insisted that you should never start to fish a sea trout pool at night until you could count seven stars wheeling above your head in the great firmament. It makes sense not to disturb a pool. It is like the temptation of a saint to stand by the pool at dusk, rod in hand, for this is the time when sea trout and salmon sport and leap.

WET FLIES

BLUE DUN
(Large Dark Olive)

BROUGHTON POINT
(Iron Blue Dun)

DARK CLARET and GROUSE

KATE MacLAREN

BLOODY KATE

MARCH BROWN

PEARLY INVICTA

GROUSE and ORANGE
(Without Kick)

GROUSE and ORANGE
(With Kick)

(Lime)

(Yellow)

(Pearl)

(Magenta)

(Orange)

SWEENY VARIANTS

NYMPHS

CORIXA (WATER BOATMAN)

(ALL SIX ABOVE) FOOTBALLER SERIES (CHIRONOMID PUPA)

GOOD NEWS NYMPH
(SEDGE PUPA)

HOGLOUSE

JACK KETCH
(WATER BEETLE)

TWO-TONE

HARES'S EAR

IRON BLUE

LARGE DARK OLIVE

MEDIUM OLIVE

PALE WATERY

PHEASANT TAIL

DAPPING FLIES

HORNED DADDY
(Crane Fly)

OLIVE DRAKE
(Mayfly Dun)

SILVER BLUE

MAYFLIES

TAYLOR'S GREEN CHAMPION

TAYLOR'S YELLOW CHAMPION

SPENT BLACK DRAKE

DRY FLIES

MINI MUDDLER

SILVERHORN

TERRY'S TERROR

DRY FLIES

DADDY LONGLEGS

DAMSEL

GINGER QUILL

HOOLET

LARGE RED SEDGE

LECKFORD PROFESSOR

MARCH BROWN

DRY SHRIMP

LURES

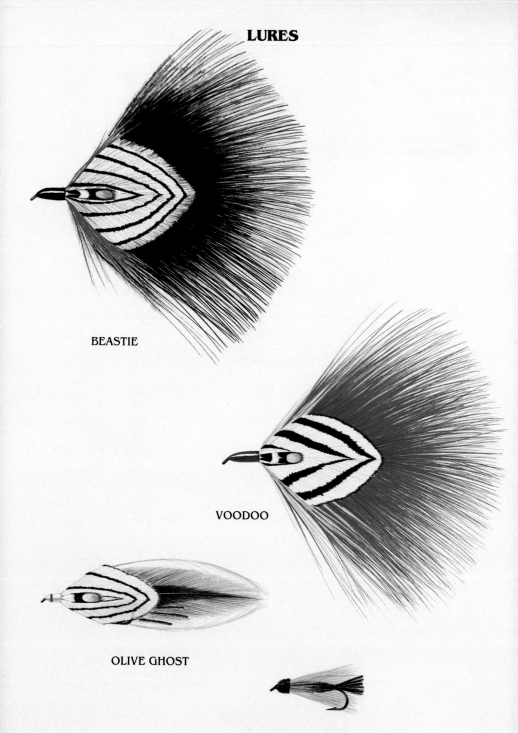

BEASTIE

VOODOO

OLIVE GHOST

GREEN AND BROWN JERSEY

SALMON and SEA TROUT FLIES

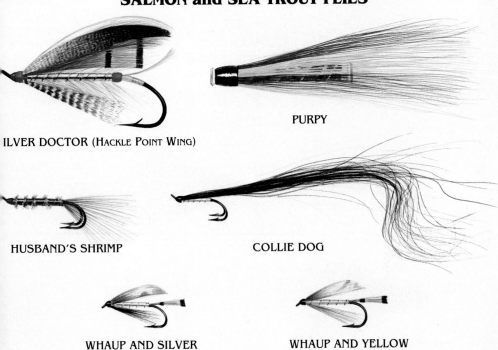

ILVER DOCTOR (Hackle Point Wing)

PURPY

HUSBAND'S SHRIMP

COLLIE DOG

WHAUP AND SILVER

WHAUP AND YELLOW

SILVER BLUE

BLACK DOCTOR (Brush Off System)

MOONLIGHT ON
MRS HIGGINGBOTHAM

THUNDER AND LIGHTNING (Sheath Wing)

SALMON TUBE FLIES

KINMONT WILLIE

LADY OF MERTOUN

MEG WITH THE
MUCKLE MOUTH

MEG IN THE BRAWS

MICHAEL SCOTT

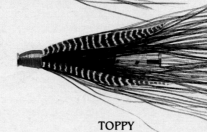

TOPPY

'A patient angler stood watching rod in hand'.

I recollect taking a stroll by the River Otter, up past the little dam which ends the estuarine part. In the top pool a goodly peal was taking his evening constitutional, cruising around and making the occasional sortie into the dusk-gathering air. A patient angler stood watching, rod in hand. It was a time of perfect stillness so holiday-makers, out for their evening stroll, were attracted by the commotion made by the leaping fish. They couldn't understand why the fisherman silently watched. They urged him to cast his fly at the fish, but he smiled and shook his head, cursing them under his breath, I imagine. Eventually, the darkness filled the valley, the passers-by melted away into the gloaming, and I, reluctantly went with them.

Sea trout fishing, especially by night, has more folk-lore attached to it than any other branch of fly-fishing. It was 'Lemon Grey' who, by his own observation, proved wrong the assumption that peal will drop back to the tail of a pool as soon as it is dark. A proportion of them will move into the runs at the head of the pool. I have always believed that sea trout would take up a position from which they could escape from a prowling otter. Alas, otter watching is a thing of the past and I am not certain if the otter finds it harder to pursue a fish through a stickle or through a deepening pool, though I suspect the former to be the case.

I started my own night fishing on the Torridge. Local advice was that the darker it was, the better the fishing. Later I found this advice challenged by another fine sea trout man, Jeffrey Bluett. In his book, *Sea Trout and Occasional Salmon* he extolled the virtues of the 'silvery nights'. My opinion is that the problem of fly-fishing by moonlight is not so much that fish see the angler and his wiles, but that temperature of water swings rapidly. Bluett was right to recommend flies with bodies of silver tinsel for fishing in bright moonlight simply because they glitter.

If I had to choose a perfect night it would be mild with a plump, orange harvest moon low over the horizon. I do not welcome the blackest of nights although I made my best catch on such a night and broke yet another of the old maxims by casting a dry-fly upstream.

This was on the River Ilen in Southern Ireland. I had taken station on a weed-bed where I could cast down and across into the head-run of the pool below. As soon as darkness fell a nasty cold wind sprang up, forcing me to turn around to cast upstream into the flat-tail of the pool above. I changed to a small Black Pennell spider which refused to sink. There was a glimmer of light shining down the pool and in its faint sheen I saw the swirl of a fish taking the fly on the surface. Before an hour had passed I had killed eleven 'white trout' and one slob which had run up with them from the estuary.

It was that night which brought home to me two dangers of night fishing. As I walked back downstream to the ford I passed a gang of half-a-dozen poachers with a net across the stream.

'Good-night, sorr,' they greeted me as I hurried by.

'Oh, those lads from Cork again,' authority told me in answer to my report.

Then, after I had been fishing for half-an-hour, the weed-bed suddenly heaved itself upwards at my feet, giving me a near heart-attack until the grinning face of a large otter appeared. It was weird that I made my best catch ever with an otter at my feet and a team of poachers below me.

It goes almost without saying that those of nervous or credulous disposition should not fish at night. A few years ago one of the widest-read sea trout experts was F. W. Holiday who was attuned to the supernatural and kept quite cheerful in the presence of ghosts, so much so that he told me he strolled back from the river once in the company of a soldier from Napoleonic times. I have had no such experiences myself, but I do not sneer at those who do, for is there not a famous pool on the Spey where a voice from an unseen source has ordered many an angler to leave the water immediately? And is there not a famous boathouse by the Tweed where anglers will not pass the night, and any who are forced to, will never venture upstairs?

'Lemon Grey' recounted the tale of an angler he accompanied to the water at night, growing so nervous that he decided to take the quaking soul back to his billet. On crossing the waterside meadow the man was so relieved that he jumped playfully onto a hummock. This turned out to be a sleeping cow which heaved itself up onto its legs, overturning the now terrified angler in the process. It does make sense for a town-dwelling angler to familiarise himself with the sounds of the countryside by night, from coughing cattle, screaming vixens, grunting badgers to the chirping of friendly grasshopper warblers. It would be sensible for some enterprising entrepeneur to make a recorded tape of such things.

A night expedition to the Cothi brought home to me more realistic dangers. The stream was clear. By day it was impossible to tempt the sea trout I could easily discern. I marked down one shoal for a night attack. I did have some misgivings for the far bank was thickly wooded with conifers and I knew it would be pitchy under those trees. I took two usual precautions. I reconnoitred the entry point to the pool and pushed a stick into the bank to which a piece of white paper had been speared. I made a cast or two by day, tying a piece of button-thread around the line where it would be between my forefinger and thumb as soon as the correct length of line was extended. I knew the fly would be in the right place.

All went well even though the night was as black as the ace-of-spades. After a couple of hours I had neither caught fish, nor seen any, so I began to edge back towards the patch of white on the bank, but instead of the water growing shallower, it began to get deeper and deeper, approaching the wader tops. Reflecting afterwards, I guessed that I had moved along a whaleback of shingle, then tried to cut across the deep gulley between the ridge and the bank. At the time, I calmed myself down, then struggled across to the far bank with the prospect of a mile walk in the dark through thickly-planted conifers. Reaching the lane, my face, lashed by the branches, I looked like a survivor from the barbed-wire entanglements of the Battle of the Somme.

One of the old saws which I hold to be true is to use the blackest fly on the darkest night. It is a device of mine to cut the eye from a wet-fly hook and to replace it with a loop of nylon, about a quarter of an inch long. The nylon is firmly whipped to the hook-shank after being crimped, and the fly body dressed over it. This can be fixed to the leader 'by feel' on the darkest of nights, either by one of those small metal snells on the tippet of the leader, or else by loop-over-loop attachment. A good night-fly for sea trout is the Connemara Black. The blue-jay hackle perhaps helps as blue is the most visible colour in diminished light.

The colour of sea trout flies is one of those delightful controversies. 'Lemon Grey' was certain that traditional teal-winged flies were of no account on the Torridge. He favoured yellow and orange. Curiously, if you read accounts of that favoured band of pre-war visitors to the Swedish Em you will learn that the same colour prejudice existed there. Now, the Em is a short river which runs out of a peat marsh into the Baltic sea. I, too, cannot give a logical explanation, but I favour the use of yellow, orange and fiery brown-bodied flies for peat-stained waters.

Charles Ritz made us envious with his accounts of the monstrous sea trout of the River Em. These fish fatten up on little herring-like fish in the Baltic which are called 'strømming'. It has been said that even bigger fish run up Russian rivers like the Vistula and now that anglers are going to Russia we shall learn if this is true. I have no doubt that the Kentish Stour once boasted runs of sea trout to equal that of the Em, the so-called Fordwich trout, but that river is but a shade of its past glory; water abstraction and commercial netting in the river in years gone by having taken their toll.

An earlier pilgrim to the Em, J. D. Greenway, was adamant that those giant fish positively detested flies with any trace of blue in their make-up. He did favour black and invented a killing fly for the river with the comical name of 'Moonlight on Mrs Higgingbotham'. The tail was of Golden Pheasant topping. He fashioned the body from a dubbing of black seal's fur with a ribbing of narrow-oval silver tinsel. His throat hackle was of black heron and with grey guinea fowl hackle in front. The silver pheasant under-wing had a strip of teal and another G. P. topping over it.

If memory serves me rightly, 'Lemon Grey' had a Labrador bitch which was his companion on night fishing expeditions. When a peal was taken, it was tossed up onto the bank. The dog would collect the fish, add it to the growing pile and protect this haul against maurauding rats and foxes. It is frustrating to try to keep Izaak Walton's commandment, 'Study to be quiet' whilst fishing in the dark. You should go to extreme lengths, say by practising to cast blindfold in the company of a friend, for as soon as you cannot see the line in the air the casting timing goes to hell. In particular, the rod's arcs in the air grow longer. You have to learn how to remove a hook by feel, and to kill a fish in the net by breaking its back. It is anathema to shine a torch near to the water. My preference is for a metal-rimmed keep-net, and if the frame is either silver or painted white, a fish can be seen as it slips safely home. My own *bête noir* is tying wind knots in the leader, so I keep a spare leader nearby — some folk wind it around a hat brim.

I try to enter the water and reach the casting place just before last light, then to wait patiently until the first stars appear. This is a trying time. Once, in a Torridge pool, a huge salmon threw himself skywards right in front of my waders. It is sensible to use a long rod with a medium-soft action. The extra length helps to keep the line clear of the bank vegetation on the back-cast. You cannot afford to crash in and out of the river at night. The use of a stiff rod would risk tearing the hook free from the notoriously soft mouth of the quarry, but also it encourages the fish to dash about and leap when you need to lead it quietly out of the run.

The trouble is that in night fishing you are alone in the darkness and all of the good books ever written cannot help you. That big catch I made on the Ilen broke all of the rules. I do have one golden rule which serves me well. I go to the place where I am going to fish. I go there by day, preferably in the morning. I work out the distance of line I will cast from the spot where I will stand, and I mark the line at that point, where it leaves the reel. I try to choose a simple target area, and by that I mean where there are no complex currents or back eddies, but a place where I know the fly will enter the water and swing round in a straightforward way. I cast to this place several times, watching to see how the line behaves and above all, how it feels until the fly comes below me on the dangle. It is important to 'groove this into muscle memory' as the golfers say. I do these things well away from the time I shall fish by night.

Although greased-line fishing for salmon with low-water flies became unfashionable, the discovery of the importance of water-temperature in relation to air temperature by Arthur Wood* should still guide our vital choice of when to fish sunk-fly or sub-surface. In my late Autumn fishing on the Tweed I'm happy if I can feel the heavy tube fly tick-ticking over the pebbles as it swings round. The salmon are so tight to the river floor that anglers swear the graze-marks on their under-jaws are caused by their rasping against the river-bed. Post-war theory has also stressed the importance of oxygen levels in the water as a guide to taking times, but whereas I find it simple enough to take air and water temperatures, I would have to draw the line at bankside chemical analysis!

Sea trout fishermen have long remarked on the phenomenon of fish taking freely for the first hour or two after nightfall, and then the fishing suddenly ceases. Of course this is sometimes due to the fish becoming satiated and then dispersing from their feeding lies. On other occasions, though, the decline in air temperatures, which can be sudden on clear nights, encourages the fish to drop further back in the runs, to take up positions in deeper water. In earlier times this would have been less of a problem for the angler, for having greased his silk line before starting to fish, as time passed, the buoyancy would have been lost and the fly would fish deeper. Nowadays we either have to change to a sinking line, which is a nuisance in the darkness, or else change the fly to one which has been weighted.

This sometimes takes the odd fish after the first feeding period has ceased, though more often than not, there are no takes until the first flush of 'false dawn' glows on the Eastern horizon. A noticeable discouragement to fish is when a white mist drifts across the river from the meadows. I have many times witnessed the dead-hand effect this had on the evening rise on the Test, and it simply means that fish cannot see flies on the surface of the water, whilst a sudden fall in temperature also happens. Fortunately, on a warm summer night these ghostly wraithes

*An expert salmon fly-fisher between the Wars who fished on the Cairnton water of the River Dee in Scotland. He discovered the technique of greased-line fishing which helps anglers catch salmon in low water and summer conditions.

disappear after the first hour or so, to reappear at dawn. 'Lemon Grey' had an ingenious way of dealing with sea trout which moved into deeper water, for he knotted-in a collar of heavy gut above his nylon leader, both materials being available in his time. This gut absorbed water faster than the nylon and provided him with a sinking leader as the first hour slipped by.

In no other method of fishing is experience more important than theory. This is because the angler is isolated from his companion by the darkness. The advice I would reiterate is to choose a pool where currents are so straightforward as to swing the fly and leader across without the 'daylight' complications of either mending line, or having to speed it up during its progress across the pool. A simple 'down and across' glide is a boon for night fishing.

It is true that, as in Bustard fishing on a river like the Eden, local experts who know their river, will move from place to place as if by the light of day. Stumbling around the banks of unknown rivers in the dark is not my cup of tea, for being a fly-rod wanderer, I never know a river that well. Night fly-fishing is, for me, an occasional exciting expedition, so I keep it as simple as I can.

There has also been a tendency in recent years to choose really big flies for sea trout, say those which are made-up on size 6 and 8 low-water hooks. My personal experience is that for the most part smaller flies work best. I usually fish with a normal size 10, or even 12 wet-fly hook. My choice of pattern is for the Teal Blue & Silver on a shiny night, almost any black fly for the darkest times, and the Grouse & Claret has been a good killer on occasion. If sedges continue to come to the river for the first hour or so, then the Invicta does sterling work. When the moon is very bright I have fished upstream with a dry-fly, and, in preference to the undoubtedly successful Bustards, I prefer either a white-winged Coachman or an Ermine Moth.

It's strange that whereas a dragged dry-fly is anathema when stalking brown trout by day on the Test, it sometimes excites sea trout to a frenzy at night. One memorable night found me throwing a muddler upstream from a beam-weir on the Teifi, then pulling it back to make a deliberate wake in the shimmering moonlit surface of the river, to have sewin chasing it with heart-stopping furrows. Ah, well, book rules are meant to be broken!

Sea Trout flies

Chapter 11
In the Footsteps of George Kelson

'Remember that you are the master and
can determine where and at what pace your
fly shall fish.'

Floating Line for Salmon & Sea Trout
Anthony Crossley

Before Kelson, salmon fly-fishing was simple. Today, modern
hairwing flies, tubes and Waddingtons have rescued it from
the complications on which George Kelson attempted to
build his reputation.

In 1845, William Scrope published his book, *Days and Nights of
Salmon Fishing*. This was to do with his experiences and exploits
of salmon fishing on the Tweed.

The Scrope flies are of simple structure, often with no hackle.
The wing was a single strip of feather, say white-tipped black turkey
or barred teal. The body was a simple dubbing of hair or wool.
Scrope listed no more than six patterns; two of these flies are of
the masculine gender, three of the feminine and one of neuter.
Angling historians recall their fascinating names. There's 'Kinmont
Willie' which was a favourite on the Annan, the main features of
which were a body of hare's ear and a wing of teal. There was 'the
Lady of Mertoun', presumably taking its name from the famous
beats near St Boswells on the Tweed where I have wetted the
occasional fly, also with a teal wing, but body of blackish water
rat's fur. 'Toppy' is next, later to be hi-jacked by Kelson, as we
shall see, dressed at that time with a wing of white-tipped turkey
and a body of black bullock's hair. 'Michael Scott' was the fourth
fly, 'a most killing wizard', followed by 'Meg with the Muckle Mouth'
and 'Meg in her Braws'. Of course these flies had added
embellishments and the full dressings are given in the appendices.

It is clear, though, that they are a far cry from the fully-dressed monstrosities which arrived a few years later and which dominated our salmon fishing for the best part of the century following, to its detriment.

Why did the complex salmon fly take over? This is hard to say, other than the fact that soldiers, traders and diplomats were starting to pile up in distant parts of the Empire and were no doubt fascinated by the exotic plumages surrounding them, samples of which they brought or sent back to Britain. Who first dreamed up the idea of marrying together strands of these feathers to make the complex wing of, say a Popham or a Childers? Again, as we shall see, Kelson claimed it for his own invention but it was recorded by writers like Francis Francis and 'Ephemera' before he arrived on the scene. All that Kelson can claim is that he played a prominent part in enshrining the fully-dressed wonders of manual dexterity into the practice of salmon fly-fishing, so much so that anglers of the day feared to go to the water without their Jock Scotts and Wilkinsons.

As we know from the legend of a billion monkeys with typewriters eventually producing a sonnet, it was obvious that one or two of these combinations of feather and silk would prove to be killing flies. Jock Scott and Silver Doctor have stood the test of time and survived into their modern hair-wing forms, but myriads of other patterns beloved of our grandfathers have simply disappeared into the mists of time. Who today would even know the dressing for such favourites of their day as the Lion, Beaconsfield or the Donkey?

We owe this tradition largely to one man, George M. Kelson and his monumental book, *The Salmon Fly*. The sad truth is that today, whenever a writer is researching material for a book on the salmon fly he rarely goes back beyond Kelson for the simple reason that it is convenient to have the information all within the covers of a single book. Unfortunately, to put it bluntly, a great deal of the information given in Kelson's book is just plain wrong. To make his reputation he simple took other peoples' ideas and inventions and re-allocated them to himself and his friends. We have already seen that Toppy was an age-old Tweed fly, described by Scrope in 1845. Kelson tarts it up somewhat, ascribed it to the Rev. A. Williams and describes it as a fly for the River Usk. And he did this over and over again.

The most notorious example was probably the Thunder & Lightning, one of the most killing patterns ever devised for salmon, and, happily, following that age-old precept of simplicity, for almost anyone can make the good old Thunder. I did some probing in

Ireland when fishing that famous Ridge Pool on the Moy with the grand old gillie, Jeff Hearns, grandson of the legendary Pat. Now Pat Hearns probably invented the Thunder & Lightning, though it could possibly have been his local friend, lesser known but equally skilled, Devanney, for the two men got their flies hopelessly mixed. Either way, the Thunder came out of the West long before Kelson was ever heard of, yet he gives it to G. S. Wright, the oracle of Sprouston on Tweed. It was no bad thing to be a friend of Kelson, your reputation would grow at a stroke of his pen!

I discussed the phenomenon of Kelson with a friend who opined that what really happened was that Kelson was envious of the reputation then being earned by Halford, with his books on dry-fly fishing, and he thought to emulate this in the world of the salmon fly, though without having to do all of that tedious research. Inevitably the muck would hit the fan sooner or later, and Kelson's reputation was effectively destroyed in his own lifetime even if sloppy researchers have restored it long after. This is the way it happened.

Kelson's book had appeared in 1895 and it was reviewed with faint praise by R. B. Marston, editor of the *Fishing Gazette* at that time. This must have caused resentment which was to surface much later. Marston, a knowledgeable man, must have detected the falsehoods in the book, but for the time being he kept quiet, perhaps waiting for better times to indulge himself in an exposure.

The explosion came in 1908 and it began with the saga of the Inky Boy, a Kelsonian invention which has long died on us. Firstly, though, it should be recalled that Kelson had a commercial turn of mind, so much so that sections of his book read like a tackle catalogue where followers of the Great Man are advised to shop all over England, buying the Kelson coat in Piccadilly; the Kelson socks in Ramsgate; the Kelson fly box in Kelso and so on. In 1907 Kelson announced in the angling press that traditional flies like the Jock Scott were now passé, the fish were used to them and were refusing them, though how this information was passed from fish to fish he didn't explain. However, he had invented a new miracle fly, the Inky Boy which was killing fish all over the place. No one should be without one. When anxious anglers set out to fill their fly boxes with the miracle fly they encountered a snag. Where could one obtain the feathers? The trouble started innocuously enough, a letter in the *Fishing Gazette* from William Baigent to this effect, to which Kelson replied that the hackle and wing feathers included plumage from tourocou crest which could only be bought from a feather merchant in Paris! The original dressing of the Inky Boy is included in the appendix. Might it occur in suspicious minds that this innocent query had been 'planted'?

The following week Kelson went on to complain that readers were bombarding him with their samples of the Inky Boy which wouldn't catch fish. He complained:

'Personally, I wouldn't dream of using any one of the samples sent, most of which are capital chub flies'. He was supported by no less an angler than John James Hardy who declared 'personally I have great faith in the fly' and all seemed well. No sign of the storm clouds gathering below the horizon. Seemingly Marston was leading Kelson into the quicksand with a gentle footnote that there was no reason why fish should refuse a fly because its dressing was slightly different to that stipulated. Kelson rose to this fly with a long letter which, in modern parlance, 'went over the top' as if he were being criticised unfairly, defending himself with such phrases as:

'but what in the name of Fortune can be the reason for throwing cold water on the infinitely more important measure of being careful and accurate in a fly for use when the most difficult conditions prevail?'

And you might think that this was not even a storm in a tea-cup without realising that Marston was preparing a pit for Kelson knowing that the man's personality would be the means to trip him into it. Next round in the game was a cartoon printed in the *Fishing Gazette* show the Inky Boy shedding tears, with the caption: 'I hope I am correctly dressed at last!'

That did it. The broadside was fired off by George Kelson's son, Reginald, pater being under the weather. He was upset by the reflection on his father. This gave Marston the opportunity for a counterblast at the wider grievance he had been harbouring over the previous fifteen years. This is how he replied:

'His (Kelson's) book is supposed to give us the history of certain salmon flies. I say that some of these he claimed to have invented or named were neither invented nor named by him . . . Kelson claimed he was the inventor of making salmon flies with mixed wings. Salmon flies with mixed wings were made before he was ever heard of or thought of . . .'

The crux of Marston's accusations was that many salmon flies claimed by Kelson for himself, his father or his friends, were known previously as was the mixed-wing style of dressing. Kelson came back with the obvious riposte — he couldn't leave well alone — name these flies! But Marston had been doing his homework otherwise why was there no action for libel by the tetchy Kelson?

Marston stated that Kelson's book laid claim to a fly called the Donkey which had earlier appeared in a book by 'Ephemera'

108

(Fitzgibbon) in 1850. This was just an opening salvo. There were three hundred standard patterns claimed by Kelson which were now called into question. Some, which we know today; the Black Dog, the Black Dose, the Bonne Bouche, the Wilkinson, were traced by Marston to other authors of over fifty years before, such as Stoddart and Paton. For good measure, Marston also took apart Kelson's claims to have invented certain hook patterns, techniques like striking from the reel, all of which had earlier been described by others.

When you're on the way up in life friends pat you on the back. It seems that they are really feeling for the soft spots for the knife to go in when you are on the way down. Other anglers now waded in with further accusations, but Kelson went on, defending the indefensible. Eventually, aware that a hatchet job had been done on his book and his reputation, he wrote plaintively:

'You (Marston) pose again as my benefactor as though the whale would pose as the protector of Jonah by inviting him to come in out of the wet . . .'

Then Marston went in for overkill, printing over several pages, two columns. The left-hand column was Kelson's claims. The right-hand column opposite each claim was a researched, irrefutable negation. He ended with the final question:

'Shall we cry quits, K?'

And Kelson had no option. Marston had cut him down with uncharacteristic cruelty when he was a comparatively old man, seemingly not in the best of health. But who did have the last word?

The sad fact is that a weekly or monthly paper is a consumer product, only of interest long-term for a few dedicated researchers, whereas a book stands for posterity. I have no doubt that Marston destroyed Kelson's reputation in his own lifetime, and when I was young I met older anglers who remembered the incident well. Yet Kelson's book remains today as a collector's piece. Modern writers go to it as a standard work, little realising that its information is blemished, and they repeat unknowingly the claims which Marston surgically exposed down to the last screaming nerve. In its day, the 'F.G.' had the muscle to put down Kelson, but I think I can still hear a wry chuckle from Kelson's tomb every time angling writers refer to his book as a standard work and, say, allocate Pat Hearn's 'Thunder' to Wright of Sprouston.

It's worth remembering, though, next time you see Kelson described as 'the father of the salmon fly' that Marston 'drowned his honour in a shallow cup and sold his reputation for a song'.

Is this long-ago squabble important today? I think it is because somewhere along the line people like Kelson changed the evolution of the salmon fly into the direction of the absurd and the complex, and this remained for years until a modern thinker like A. H. Wood began to mull over the mechanics of fishing to the extent that he was able to use a simple pattern like the low-water March Brown throughout a season without any apparent diminution of catches. The final irony is that today we have returned to the eighteenth century simplicity of fly structure, the pre-Kelsonian Tweed flies, inheritors of Toppy and Meg-in-her-Braws. Historically, that would make Scrope the Master, and I would go along with that.

I have said before that salmon fly-fishing is a business of mechanics, lacking the intellectual elements of trout fishing. True, there are occasional discussions on whether or not salmon take food in fresh water, and whilst the accepted opinion is that they do not, because their digestive organs have atrophied for the long journey upstream, I join that minority which believes that at least they derive some benefit from crushing certain soft things to absorb the juices, but that's not provable. There is, too, field for fruitful speculation as to why they take a fly in the river. Some argue for curiosity, some for the predatory instinctive reaction to colour and movement, but my belief is that it is a response to sea-memory, perhaps of the krill which salmon feed on in Northern waters. It may be simply enough to know that salmon will take a fly and that the 'how' and 'when' are more important than why.

Is it mere cynicism to assert that the number of really 'good' books on salmon fishing are very few? And by 'good' I mean books which throw new light on the subject. Is it cynical to say that compared to trout fishing literature, salmon writing is often poor and confused? We shall see. Fly-fishing is a sport which depends very much on its literature to transmit ideas. Books are important to our sport.

After Kelson there were no landmarks in salmon fly-fishing until the time of A. H. Wood when the theory of greased-line fishing was written up by Wood's disciple, Anthony Crossley in his book *The Floating Line for Salmon and Sea Trout*. It is almost true to say that before Wood the standard technique was to fish down and across the river with a sinking line and fully-dressed salmon fly in various sizes. Wood discovered that under summer conditions, salmon would accept a fly fished just below the surface of the water on a floating line. Obviously, in his time before the last war, Wood had to grease a silk line to make it float as modern plastic lines did not exist.

In its basic form, Wood's idea was that salmon took a fly high in the water when the water was warm, and they took it deep in the water when it was cold. It's generally accepted that the dividing line is a temperature of forty-five degrees Fahrenheit. I guess that today most anglers carry a thermometer and their choice between floating and sinking line would depend on that temperature reading.

It wasn't as simple as that for it's a quirk of human nature that we must complicate everything! Wood maintained that the essential factor for the greased line technique was that the air temperature should exceed that of the water. The funny thing is that once you start to carry thermometers around salmon rivers you notice bizarre shifts in relative temperatures, especially in those fine fishing months of March/April and September/October. Thus, according to Wood, it wouldn't matter if the water were a few degrees below the magical forty-five, if the air was warmer, then floating line should be employed.

Now, Crossley's book is interesting and important for the salmon angler to read, but, it has to be said, Wood, and hence his pupil Crossley, used words in a peculiar way, so much so that I have had to read passages several times to make sense of them. An example is when Wood talks of a low water fly 'floating' downstream. The immediate impression is that he is discussing a dry-fly, but that must be nonsense. He is talking of a sub-surface fly coming downstream without drag. Drag was anathema to Wood and he insisted that the fly should come downstream 'like a dead thing', that is completely inert.

This is difficult to accomplish, which is why no one fishes that way today. It was achieved in two ways, firstly by casting across the river, even somewhat upstream, and by frequently mending the line in an upstream direction to mitigate the effects of the current. Wood also insisted that these upstream mends should be executed in such a way as to avoid the fly being moved in the water. The only way to do this is to push the rod forwards and away from the body before making the upstream switch. It does work, I've tried it.

Let me digress. Although Wood started a new school of fly fishing for salmon, the use of lightly dressed drab flies was not unknown before, notably in Spey patterns like the Lady Caroline. Such flies were designed for the streamy waters of Speyside, they were dressed on finer wire hooks than the normal 'ordinary forged' irons, unfairly called 'meat hooks'. Spey flies were tied on longer-shanked hooks of a thinner wire called 'Dee' hooks, so in a way the greased line method grew out of an older tradition. To make his flies work just below the surface of the water Wood eventually had his patterns dressed on fine-wire hooks which today we call 'low water'. He preferred to use single hooks, believing that doubles, with their larger heads, would skate on the surface of the water. The dressing of his flies was skimpy, the modified body occupying no more than half, perhaps even a third of the shank with a whisp of hackle and a slim, low wing — such were the low water flies. Nor was the pattern important to him. He might well fish a whole season with just two patterns in various sizes, Blue Charm and March Brown.

It was not long before reaction set in, some pointing out that Wood fished a special water, his Cairnton fishery on the Dee, where conditions suited his methods. The important thing is that he went back to the physical basics of salmon fishing and rethought them from basic principles and with an enquiring mind. In my opinion, this did not happen again for decades until Reg Righyni took it a stage further in his two books, *Salmon Taking Times* and *Advanced Salmon Fishing*. It is strange, too, that both Wood and Righyni were not natural writers. Wood wrote no book and Righyni is often obscure in his use of words.

It is sad, too, that Anthony Crossley, the Boswell to Wood's Johnson, came to grief just as the war was looming. He was one of that lucky band of British anglers who fished for the giant sea trout on the River Em in Southern Sweden. Hurrying over there to enjoy one last season before the shooting match was to begin, he died in a plane crash. It is true that few, if any anglers now fish the classical 'Wood' way but his contribution to our knowledge of the way salmon behave in relation to the fly is enormous, whether we realise it or not. Righyni added to this advance in thought of the importance of water temperatures with the equal importance of light values and changing oxygen content.

I decided one day on the Findhorn to fish the classical greased-line method, albeit with a modern floating line. At first sight the choice of river was far from perfect, for of all the rivers I know, the Findhorn is the least typical. For one thing the fish are spooky like trout and they have to be stalked with care. Careless approach sets them bolting to cover. Then the river is virtually a spate stream, rising and falling rapidly according to rain, and in its low state, the fish tend to be stiff. This caused the local rods to pay little attention to normal practice. One expert I know will succeed in taking salmon in low water conditions by fishing a heavy tube fly on a fast-sinking line at night.

The water was low and clear, the weather the best of July sunshine which cooked-up that rocky gorge into a windless heat-trap. As hour after fruitless hour passed by I told myself 'greased

A classical Durham Ranger

line! A likely story'. By early evening I was simply going through the motions when I came to a pool called 'the Whins'. The water here was compressed into a rocky channel, deep, fast and even. Recollecting that Wood had said, in one of his letters, that he never despaired of a pool down to fifteen feet deep, I swam the fly down from an upstream cast. When it was opposite to me, and I could clearly see it just below the surface of the pool, drifting downstream 'like a dead thing', as Crossley would have it, then suddenly a great salmon, unknown to me till then, porpoised up from the secret depth of the pool to hit the fly with enormous shock. Being by then quite bereft of hope and concentration, I reacted by jerking my rod upwards as if hitting a wild brown trout, taking the fly away from the salmon.

One of the old London street cries from the days when the City boasted of up to twenty tackle shops was:

'Bad tackle is the angler's bane.

A straight rod buy in Crooked Lane'.

Crooked Lane has long since gone, and perhaps Skues, Marryat and Halford would have their rods fashioned there by the skilled craftsmen of Eaton & Deller. The doggerel is not entirely true, for in the days of Kelson and Murdoch, a salmon fly rod for Spey casting would be made deliberately with an upturned curve to its tip, a retroussé effect. And it worked, for those old-time casters would throw some forty yards with such rods.

George Kelson did have one claim to fame. He was probably the first writer to illustrate and describe specialised casts for salmon fishing. His 'Governor's cast' brings a smile to the lips. It was intended to solve the problem of throwing a long line in a confined space. The line was stretched out behind the angler and attached to a post by a rubber band. A gillie or servant attended to this post. Then, with a mighty snatch the line broke free from the post and was propelled forward by the rod.

When a trout angler first takes up the double-handed rod he finds little difficulty in mastering the simple overhead cast. The Spey and Double Spey casts tend to bemuse him, so much so that I know many an occasional salmon angler who has never attempted these casts which are essential when, as is often the case, there are high banks or trees behind to block the back-cast. It is sad because the two Spey casts are quite simple to learn. They are simply roll casts, and the only difficulty is in positioning the fly so that the straightforward roll cast can be performed.

It's lovely to work a little mystique into the business of fishing, and instructors make their living from this belief that the Spey cast is as tricky as a perfect golf swing. In fact, the average intelligent person should be able to master it within a quarter of an hour, given competent tuition. The 'roll' part of the cast is about the easiest action to learn in all fishing, as it is just the bowling of line forwards by cutting down with the rod tip. Once that is done it only remains to put the fly in the right place for the roll cast. The fly should be positioned upstream of you for the Single Spey and downstream of you for the Double Spey. If it's directly in front of you it's likely to leave the water like a bullet and hit you in the face!

All casters agree that you need to be surrounded by water to make good Spey casts, for the adhesion of the line to the water is necessary to bring out the action of the rod. As luck would have it, I fished a beat at Yair House on the Tweed where the bank was too high behind for overhead casting, but the water in front was too deep for wading. Happily, Bob Findlay, gillie of the Tilbouries beat on the Dee, had developed a version of the Double Spey cast to overcome a similar problem on his fishery. Almost impossible to describe in words, the first upstream movement of the line is followed by a short, sharp flip which turns the rod upside down with the reel drum facing heavenwards. This dumps the fly and line rather untidily directly in front of the caster from which position he can make a normal roll cast.

Another curiosity is the alarm felt by the occasional salmon angler when he first has to Spey cast with a heavy tube-fly and sunk line. As he bends into the line-retrieve after the fly has worked downstream onto 'the dangle', he feels as if he's dragging the fly through a sea of glue, and then the fly suddenly accelerates as it approaches the surface and shoots back at the angler with the speed and venom of a stray bullet. It's quite amusing to watch. The remedy is to continue the line haul into a downstream roll cast to clear the fly from the water in a safe way.

When a salmon fly-fisher has learned to put out a long line with the two Spey casts he usually abandons the overhead throw if only because he ceases to be plagued with wind-knots.

Chapter 12
Fashions and Flies

'I believe myself that simply dressed flies
made of comparatively few materials would
kill just as well as some of these
complicated patterns which involve the use
of feathers from half-a-dozen different birds
in addition to several various coloured silks
and two or three different sorts of tinsel.'

Salmon Fishing on the Wye J. Arthur Hutton

It's strange that anglers arriving at Inverness regard it as the
gateway to the great salmon rivers beyond, the Helmsdale,
Halladale and Thurso. In the eighteenth century, Lord Howard
raised his Kentish regiment of foot to march behind William, Duke
of Cumberland to the slaughter of Culloden. It struck my mind that
a Weldishman of that time would have been as unfamiliar with the
wild landscape beyond the Spey as a Highlander would have been
on encountering the desert sands in Kitchener's Nile campaign.

Since the days of the Jacobite rebellion people have found profit
in covering vast tracts of land with dense plantations of Sitka
spruce which acidifies the soil and squeezes out daylight. Wildlife
vanishes and I am reminded of those lines by Keats, 'and no birds
sing'. The furrowing of land which accompanies forestry makes the
rain water run off so quickly into the rivers so that spates replace
the gradual level fall-offs of yesteryear. The salmon and sea trout
have to follow the rules which Man has made for the river, running
up to spawn in short, fast spurts.

The days before the fateful Battle of Culloden saw the Jacobite
Army encamped at Inverness whilst the Hanoverians lay to the
East, at Nairn and Forres. The Master of Ordnance in the
Hanoverian Army was worried about the falling rain in case it

caused his cannon-wheels to bog down in the moorland which stretched between the two armies. I suppose he cursed the sound of raindrops drumming on the canopy of his tent. I used to think of this as I lay, half-asleep, in the cottage I rented with the Findhorn fishing at Dulsie Bridge. For the Findhorn is really a spate river.

I confess that I wasn't listening to the tramp of ghostly armies, nor the creaking of gun carriages. I was aching to hear the fevered rataplan of raindrops on the roof, for that would mean the salmon would run, fresh fish in a taking mood.

Now this part of the Findhorn is a steep gorge where one climbs down a narrow zig-zag path to the river far below. One hand grimly holds on to the wire fence, the other grips the bundle of nets and rods. The river is imprisoned between high walls of stone so that rain, higher up in the hills, brings its own special bore-wave thundering down on the unwary angler. Many is the tale of the fisherman, preoccupied with his sport until a strange and ominous roaring sound penetrates his consciousness, and, on glancing behind him he's petrified to see a great wall of water bearing down on him. Anglers usually scamper to safety in the nick of time, and ashen-faced they watch the flood rush by, bearing debris on its crest, dead sheep, farm gates, dead branches. Yet here is 'Deadman's Pool'. The water-watcher tells you that here the sun may shine, you feel at peace with the World, but, unknown to you, the high moors have been deluged with rain and you must always keep one ear cocked for that dull, muted, angry roar in the distance.

The Findhorn has its own strange ways. Of all rivers, it alone gives up its salmon when the water is still almost black from floodwater. It is the only river I know where salmon must be stalked like trout, where the carelessly heavy footfall sends them scampering for cover like frightened sheep. Here you may not enquire whether you should Spey cast or use the overhead throw. You get your line out anyway you can whilst crouching for cover behind rocks. You switch your rod, wiggle line onto the water, catapult it from the rod tip, for in the gorge you are always on top of your quarry, and all the while you must bide so quietly that a gently doe will delicately sip water from the river on a grassy shelf of the opposite bank.

I sometimes wonder if that famous angler, Francis Francis, fished for salmon in just about every river in Britain for in his book on angling he not only lists flies for the different fisheries, but he also quizzed landowners and anglers along the banks for special dressing. His patterns for the Findhorn favour purple, a colour I have long thought to be underrated by the modern angler. It's bizarre that we should associate certain patterns with certain rivers. Tweed has its Comet, for example. Tweed also favours the Whitewing, a tube-hairwing version of an old, traditional Border pattern, but, strangely, the dressing of Whitewing favoured on Lower Tweed, with its red, white and blue bunches of bucktail, differs from the fly of the same name used higher up which has a circlet of white hair with one or two strands of black mixed in.

The trouble is that these fashions rarely last. You may find one year that everyone is fishing the Willie Gunn, but next year a shrimp fly is all the rage. It means that someone has broken the mould by making a significant capture on a different pattern to that being fished by other anglers. In this way are fashions made.

This is really a question of the 'Survival of the Fittest' in evolutionary terms. An example of this is provided by that famous angler of yesteryear, Mr W. Murdoch. Long before Arthur Wood solved the problem of catching salmon in low, bright water with his floating line techniques, the problem had exercised the mind of Mr Murdoch, and although he was still imprisoned in his mind by the long, sunk-line cast downstream, he invented a series of flies for catching salmon, grilse and sea trout on bright days in summer. Five of these patterns rejoiced in the following names: Green Peacock, Golden Wasp, Golden Blue, Fail-Me-Never, and a Green Peacock Variant. It's unlikely that an angler today would be familiar with any of these flies, they have simply failed to stand the course. But the fly which headed the list, the Blue Charm, has become one of the most famous and useful patterns in the salmon angler's armoury.

The Blue Charm broke with the prevailing tradition in 1891 when Murdoch published his list, for instead of the complex wing, it simply showed to the fish a strip of dark brown mallard surmounted by a narrow strip of barred teal. It satisfied the accepted rule that a fly for use in bright, clear water should be rather drab. When feather wings gave way to the currently popular fashion of hair, the Blue Charm became the Hairy Mary. The mallard and teal feathers were replaced by brown squirrel tail. I know many anglers who prefer to use the commoner grey squirrel tail, for its three bars of colour ending in white tips are tantalisingly attractive in the stream.

I imagine that a majority of fly-fishers would include Blue Charm, or Hairy Mary, in their half-dozen favourites, flies they would not wish to be without if restricted in choice. It's amazing that it has progressed from a fully-dressed fly on a standard ordinary forged iron through to the low water version favoured by Arthur Wood, then on to the tubes, Waddingtons and long-shanked treble-hook

'. . . in this way are fashions made'.

versions invented by the late Esmond Drury. It swims in British and Irish rivers, in the torrents of Norway and North America. A companion fly, the Green Charm was forgotten almost as soon as it was invented.

In the winter of 1890 salmon anglers voted on which six flies were the most popular for angling in Scotland. The result of the survey, printed in the *Fishing Gazette*, was as follows: Jock Scott (37 votes), Silver Doctor (33), Butcher (22), Childers (19), Blue Doctor (17), Silver Grey (13). Forty-four of the best salmon anglers were invited to take part in this poll. The runners-up included two favourites of mine, the Thunder & Lightning and the Black Doctor, on which, coincidentally, I have lost fish estimated at over twenty pounds! The Editor of the old *F.G.* concluded:

> 'One lesson may be learned from this, that if an angler is about to fish a pool which another person has already fished, he had better use any other fly than a Jock Scott.'

A curiosity of the poll was that some twenty experts voted for the Jock Scott as their first choice of fly, yet today, although it is probably dressed and used still, it no longer holds paramount place.

The origin of the Jock Scott is curious in that it's the only fly invented at sea! The story is that the fly takes its name from one, Jock Scott, a servant of Lord John Scott, who, whilst accompanying his master on a sea voyage to Norway for salmon fishing, passed the time in his cabin by making up a few inventive flies for the coming campaign. The sea was so stormy that Jock was upbraided by his master for 'tying flies when you ought to be saying your prayers.' This was in the year 1845, but Jock kept this first-ever version of his fly, dressed that same night. Eventually it turned up in 1888 attached to a label, which read:

> 'The original Jock Scott, dressed by Jock Scott in 1845, when on his way to Norway in the service of Lord John Scott. Given to John G. K. Young, of Glendoune by Captain Erskine of Friars Hall, Melrose, in 1888.'

Having seen a reproduction of this fly, I was struck by the modern aspect of the dressing, in the shortness of the wing and the sparseness of the hackle which was tied in at the throat only. The fashion of later years was to add a doubled body hackle and embellish the wings.

There's no doubt that the combination of black and yellow is attractive, as witness the Jeannie.

I cannot trace any comparable poll of modern salmon anglers. The tendency of the angling press today is to titillate the public's palate with the 'flavour of the month' fly. Curiosity, though, impelled me to open my own salmon fly box and to lay it alongside the 1890 list. Which fly do I automatically plump for? I conjure up in the mind's eye a misty day on the Tweed. Autumn is giving way to winter, the leaves have stopped whirling down from the woodlands to impale themselves infuriatingly on the hook points. The river has fallen to normal level from the rains of the previous week. The colour of the water is good, clear though with the slightest greeny-brown tinge. The air is crystal-cold under a cloudless sky of high barometric pressure, and when I leave the water tonight I know the rod will have a coating of ice . . . what fly? Almost without thinking, my fingers flutter over a two-inch weighted Willie Gunn tube. That fly would have been unknown in 1890 even though another Gunn, Donald, a famous Scottish Gillie was known for his eccentric and barely literate letters in the *Fishing Gazette*. The three colours of hair which make up the wing of the Willie Gunn need to be mixed painstakingly and this is a modern equivalent of the married fibres of the Jock Scott, and almost as irritating to make. Yes, one problem of comparing lists a century apart is that in 1890 seasonal choices between summer and winter fishing would have mattered less.

Willie Gunn tubes lie next to Monro's Killer and Silver Stoat. The normal Stoat's Tail in small sizes are there for the lowest and brightest conditions. Two bright flies are stand-bys for coloured water; the Garry with its scarlet and yellow plume, and the Esmond Drury 'General Practitioner', that substitute for the 'red chap' when prawn is forbidden but the water is peaty. And there's one fly which spans the century, the Thunder & Lightning, which appeared in the list of runners-up in 1890, though mine is in modern hair-wing guise.

The 'bright day, bright fly' (or its converse) argument has raged over the years between these two lists. Mr Murdoch would never use a Silver Doctor save on a bright, sunny day, thinking that it's tinselled body would reflect the sunlight, perhaps like a small, silver prey-fish. Remembering that Miss Ballantyne was to catch her record salmon on a dace fish-bait, this made sense. My own choice for those days when the ripples actually sparkle is a tiny silver stoat. On one occasion, fishing the head of the Lawson pool on the Scottish Dee, I anticipated a grilse was likely to be enjoying the oxygen being swirled into the run at the top of this very long pool, and so I drifted a size sixteen silver stoat down through the current. I'm sure that if the ghost of Arthur Wood had been attracted downstream from his Cairnton water near Glassel, then he would have smiled his approval as I mended line feverishly to overcome drag on this tiny fly. On the Tuesday of my week a grilse took an eager snatch at the fly, but it came adrift. The weather did not change, an angler on the far bank told me that daytime fishing was a waste of time. On the Friday evening I returned, waiting for the sun to dip into a haze above the horizon so that its rays down the river into the eyes of the fish, would be diminished. The same grilse came to the fly with fervour, was played and netted. I could imagine that silver spark, glittering and weaving through the ripple so that the angry grilse could hardly resist launching itself at the annoying intruder.

I was tempted to believe that our salmon fishing forefathers missed a great deal because they had little technique to cope with low, bright water. The greased line wasn't known until the thirties. Modern floating lines were a post-war invention. We fail to understand how rivers have changed. In Murdoch's time rivers retained their water for longer periods of time because widespread furrowing and fast drainage didn't exist. Imagine how a motorway or airfield runway prevents natural seepage of rain into the ground over vast areas. See how forestry channels surface water quickly into river courses. Today, water hurries to the sea and for good salmon fishing we need frequent rainfall. Murdoch's rivers held water and fish far longer so he didn't need to throw a tiny fly into a meagre ripple at the head of a run where a grilse was gasping for oxygen. If he had needed it, then I'm sure he was clever enough to have done it. Of course, like all salmon anglers everywhere, he must have prayed for rain, but he didn't need so much, so often, for his fishing, lucky man!

From the experience of these salmon flies, invented by Mr Murdoch, it's obvious that the consistent fish-takers, like the Blue Charm, become firm favourites, generation after generation, and the others fall out of popular use. A similar story can be told about the Pennell series of flies.

The Black Pennell is undoubtedly one of the most popular patterns for lake trout fishing. It was introduced by its inventor, H. Cholmondeley-Pennell, as one of a series of flies for fishing Irish Lakes, and he described these flies in 1890. They were originally intended for sea trout fishing. The one which has stood the test of time, the Black Pennell is usually dressed sparsely. The original pattern had a tail of mixed golden pheasant tippet and topping, though today it's invariably dressed without the topping. The body is slimly made from black floss silk. The inventor also ribbed it 'thickly with a broadish silver oval' though again, today, a narrow ribbing is customary. This ribbing was given two or three turns under the tail, an embellishment which today is also omitted. The hackle was, and still is, from a black cockerel, and most anglers rightly prefer a sparse winding of two turns, choosing a bright feather with a longish fibre. Its inventor wrote: 'This fly I have always used myself as a dropper'.

Cholmondeley-Pennell's other great fly for sea trout, which is occasionally still used, is the Claret Pennell. The tail is the same as for the black version, the body of reddy-claret seal's fur, well picked out. The ribbing is also of oval silver, and, again, having two or three turns taken under the tail fibres before being wound up the body, diagonally. The hackle is of black cock. The inventor claimed this fly to be the best tail fly he had ever used for sea trout on the lakes of Connemara, and he added that it was not much use as a dropper.

Two other 'Pennells' in this collection, intended mainly for brown trout, have virtually vanished from the fly-fisher's armoury. They are the red and yellow versions. It's rewarding to know that Cholmondeley-Pennell had a practical angler's approach to fly dressing which meshes in well with modern thinking.

The bodies of his flies should be made 'thinner than thicker'. The bodies of the flies should not be carried too far towards the bend of the hook. The tail whisks should be as long as the body of the fly. The hackles should be of the same length, and he stressed the importance of the fibres standing out at all-but right-angles to the hook. All hackles should be cock. In passing, the flies were named as 'Hackle Black', 'Hackle Claret' etc, and only took their author's name later on.

It's plain common sense that a fly pattern stands the test of time simply because it's a good 'nailer' as they used to say in times gone by. The Black Pennell is as popular today as it was over a century ago and this is because the combination of black and silver, dressed as a hackled fly and fished as a dropper, copies hatching buzzers, snails, various aquatic beetles, black terrestrials which have become trapped in the surface film. It is why similar colour combinations of the same structure, William's Favourite and Kate MacLaren, also succeed, while if you go back through the entire history of fly-fishing, black and red stand out as the killing colours.

Although attempts have been made to list the most popular half-dozen trout flies, this has proved to be impossible because of the regional differences in fly-fishing methods. For myself, I know that on any loch North of Inverness I would want the Grouse & Claret as my point fly. This fly is less popular than its 'doppelganger', the Mallard & Claret, yet I prefer it because the grouse wing is sturdier than the barred mallard. I like to follow the ancient practice of darkening down the claret body dubbing by mixing in a smidgeon of mole's fur. It's curious that, notwithstanding its popularity, it has always been difficult to relate either of these two artificials to a natural insect, though for my money they take best of all when black buzzers are hatching. Certainly the few genuinely claret-coloured still-water day flies are too sparsely distributed to account for their success.

I would dislike being without a winged Greenwell whilst fishing any lake in Britain. There's no difficulty in relating this fly to the numerous pond and lake olive duns which are widespread throughout the land. I described in my book *Fly Fishing Tactics on Still Water* how I took a respectable brown trout from Blagdon lake on a size 12 Greenwell, and how that self-same fly was sent to a friend in Alabama who went on to catch a nice striped bass with it in the Cahaba river.

When the fly first became popular in the early years of this century there was some slight suggestion that Canon W. T. Greenwell was not the true originator of the fly. It was implied that the famous fly-tyer of Sprouston, James Wright had actually designed it for the Canon. This isn't true, the pattern was the Canon's and in a letter dated 27th May 1905 to his good friend, R. B. Marston, he scribbled as a footnote, 'The original dressing of the Glory is inside of a blackbird wing, coch-y-bondhu hackle, tied with yellow silk.' Canon Greenwell was then an octogenarian and planning his next fishing trip!

I must confess that I do not dress my own Glories strictly to the Canon's prescription. I like to use the primrose coloured silk tying thread, but toned down to a sort of dirty-olive colour by rubbing it with a piece of brown bees-wax. The ribbing is of fine gold wire and the hackle is a light Greenwell hen. It's a paradox that the hackle stipulated by Canon Greenwell would be much darker red with black roots and tips whereas the 'wrong' one which bears his name is ginger with black base . . . such are the mysteries of fly dressing.

Canon Greenwell confessed in this letter to Marston that he began fishing at the age of thirteen in the Browney, a small tributary of the Wear. He was born in 1820, and he wrote in 1905: 'Last year my best day was fifty-two trout, and my largest — a fario — 4 lb 2 oz.'

This question always crops up on angling Brains Trusts: 'If you had to choose one fly to use for the rest of your life what would it be?' Not fair, really, but make it a wet-fly team for trout, no problem for me. Point fly — Grouse & Claret, middle fly — Greenwell's Glory, and on the bob — the Black Pennell.

Black Pennell

Chapter 13
My Salmon Way

꧁꧂

'Wood's remark that he usually cast slightly
upstream with a slack line and that his fly
"drifted down like a dead thing" and
sometimes awash has been quoted to me
so often that I wish the book had never
been written . . .'

'Lemon Grey' in *Torridge Fishery*,
describing *Floating Line for Salmon & Sea
Trout* by Anthony Crossley

It is curious that so many trout fishermen believe that salmon
fishing is costly, whereas the beats which I fish cost little more
than the same amount of time afloat on a reservoir. The
problem is that the regular writers on salmon fishing have access
to the best fisheries and phrases like 'popping down to Tulchan'
trip glibly off the pen.

One of my haunts on the Tweed is relatively inexpensive
because the entire stretch has a forested high bank behind and, at
normal height, water up to the arm-pits in front. It necessitates the
double-Spey cast along its length, but it is usually rich in salmon,
lying towards the middle of the river and within easy reach. To
such places you can add the numerous stretches of association
water, such as at Grantown-on-Spey, and there are the lesser rivers.
My occasional forays after the king of fishes mean I've become an
expert on the cheapest salmon fishing places.

I make no apology for that, because if you can coax the
occasional fish from association waters or rivers which either hold
poor stocks or have deterrent factors such as either a fast run-off
from rain or a nauseating taint of peat, well, then you can take fish
anywhere. As a club angler on the Tweed once remarked to me:

'We get the same fish as Lord Home. They've got to get upstream and they can't go by road or rail'.

It cannot be denied that to catch fish in lesser rivers and beats you have to be a better angler than someone who is turned loose on the best pools of Dee, Tay, Tweed or Spey. This challenge has never worried me, for I delight in the fishing. As for the salmon, I don't like to eat them anyway and I give mine away when I'm lucky enough to catch one. I'd rather eat a properly smoked kipper.

You also have to be good at reading the water, for it's unlikely that a deferential gillie will attend, indicating the lies at different heights of water and pointing out the vantage casting places for your attack. This has been the story of my fishing life and it goes right back to my first salmon on the River Torridge which hit a small teal, blue and silver fly intended for one of the schoolie peal in low summer water. I stared aghast at the fast-emptying spool of my reel as the fish made tracks upstream for the distant moors. It was a chapter of accidents which ended joyfully. Seeing the water so low, the sun so hot and bright, the landlord allowed me to try for sea trout in the famous Ash Tree Pool at Torrington. I had to use my single-handed nine footer and was confined to trout flies. Casting across the current, on the retrieve the fly was hit with strong force and off went the fish. For a few seconds I was struck by paralysis, never before having had my backing run off with such speed. Then I dimly realised that the fish was dashing towards a tree which had fallen athwart the river, and just in time I applied the pressure to turn it. There followed a succession of runs, turns, attempts to gain the far bank, until after an age, the fish was wallowing in the water at my feet, though with the current trying to work it back to the trees at the end of my length of clear bank. I could see from the tip of its snout to the great sweep of its tail that it would never fall into the trout net which I was carrying. All I could do was to describe my predicament to two elderly ladies who were walking a dog by the riverside. I implored them to request the aid of another angler I had seen on a lower pool.

They disappeared, but minute followed despairing minute without help arriving. Taking my courage in both hands, I backed the enormous tail into my miniscule landing net and heaved the whole thing onto the bank. At that moment assistance arrived.

'Sorry I'm late, I was into a fish myself,' he told me.

The pitfall for the trout angler, when he turns himself loose on a salmon river is in striking. Whenever I took a trout fisherman onto a salmon river for the first time, I used to teach him the adapted words of an old music-hall ballad:

'Never, never, never strike a salmon.
You'll be sorry if you do!
You'll find one day, much to your dismay,
It will make a monkey out of you!'

Alas, no matter how many times he tells himself not to do it, when the 'take' comes suddenly the trout man reacts as if conditioned by Pavlov, with a sudden upsweep of the rod, only to feel a momentary sensation of immense and tantalising weight on the end of the line before it goes slack.

Another controversy, isn't it, how and when to hit a taking salmon? There are two basic ways and many combinations of them. The first is to hold the rod at a low angle with a loose loop of line to feed to the moving fish. The classic books tell us that when this slack line is given to the fish it forms a downstream loop of line which pulls the fly into the corner of the salmon's mouth for a wonderful hook-hold in the 'scissors' of the jaw. It's enough to give a trout man the horrors, the thought of chucking out loose line to a taking fish, and the only time I tried it, when I tightened up the fish wasn't there. I use the other method, which is also a discipline against the reactive snatch, and that is to hold the rod high. When the take comes I simply lower the rod tip as the fish moves back to its lie, fly in mouth. Then I tighten up. This works for me.

This is a good time to examine some of the nightmares which trout men experience when first turning to salmon. The first worry is simply the size and weight of the gear, and many an angler, seeing that he could easily put a fly across the river with a single-handed trout rod, asks: 'Why that big two hander?' And he may well cite American heroes like Lee Wulff who rarely used anything longer than eight feet. It's not simply a matter of casting. It's to do with line and fly management, the way the fly hangs in the water.

I recollect well the time I first experienced that terrifying phenomenon known as the 'drowned' line which never happens in trout fishing. Typical of it is when hooking a fish on the far side of a fast run and this fish dashes quickly upstream leaving you with a great downstream loop of sunken line being battered by the current. I was thunderstruck to see my line being dragged back to the sea, with the rod being forced round with it, yet a surging, leaping fish going up river in the opposite direction seemingly without any way of stopping it.

This first happened to me when fishing club water on the Border Esk. The night before it rained, and, being March, this brought up a spring run of big fish. It also brought out the local anglers who formed fishing queues on the famous Cauldron and Willows pools, so that I decided to hike upstream towards Canonbie to fish the

Nook and the Long Pool. On the way I passed the small Burn Pool which occasionally holds a fish in high water. Indeed, a fish showed as I passed and I marked him down for attention on my return. I duly fished the higher pools without any result and late afternoon found me swimming my inch-long hairwing Thunder in the Burn pool, with the late afternoon sun glinting redly through light flurries of snow. Second cast, the fish took and was away to the far side, then it made this long run with my line drowned in the intervening heavy flow. I had made the mistake of coming out of the water onto the high bank, and so I lost my first really big springer. I have since learned to discount the usual advice immediately to come out of the water, to play the fish from the land, for the golden rule to avoid the drowned line is to work as close to the fish as you can.

The experience helped me later when fishing the Ridge Pool on the Moy where the fly is often cast and taken on the far side of a central current and to dash back immediately onto dry land would be a mistake.

The trout man may also be thrown by the simplicity of fly choice in salmon work. It is more important to carry a range of sizes than a range of patterns. The size of the fly is merely its weight, to be chosen by the conditions of the water, its height, speed and temperature. True, past writers have tried to inject an intellectual element into colour and pattern, but as Wood proved, it's largely enjoyable nonsense. Obviously, you need a brightly coloured fly to show up in stained water, and orange or yellow are indicated. I carry a pattern with a silver-tinsel body for clear water and bright sunlight, the Silver Stoat being my favourite. I also like a dull pattern for dull days with clear water, the Hairy Mary, that hair-wing version of the Blue Charm, is preferred. It's important to carry an all-black fly such as the Stoat's Tail. Then I have in my box some patterns like Munro's Killer and the good old Thunder just because I like them, the best reason of all.

I have an idiosyncracy. I still like to fish with the great 'meathooks' of yore, the fully dressed irons of 2/0 and 3/0, though I dress them as hairwings. This is mostly for sunk-line work in deep water, and on one occasion the big fly hooked a fish when it shouldn't have done so. I was invited to join a firm's party for the purpose of testing a new range of salmon fly rods. I remarked that I would try a rod with a heavy sunk line and one of my 3/0 Black Doctors. It was summer, the water was warm. One of the pools on this part of the South Esk had been marked on the map by a previous visitor, 'don't bother!' So I elected to fish the fly down this pool to try the rod's ability to master cold, Spring conditions. In the thrashing I gave it the leader collected a wind-knot or two which I didn't bother to unravel. Making a very long throw downstream, to my astonishment I received a powerful take from a heavy fish which almost immediately broke me on the wind-knot.

Now, this large fly is not as impractical as you might think. I have the unproveable impression that it swims in a more attractive way than the modern tubes and Waddingtons. The other thing is that it's the only fly to avoid the frustration of catching fallen leaves in Autumn on tree-lined rivers like the Tweed. Before dressing the fly, I whip in a length of light nylon at the tail end of the hook. The fly is made in the usual way, but before wing and hackle are tied in, the nylon is looped under the hook and whipped in at the eye. The loop thus formed is strong enough to brush aside sunken leaves but not obtrusive enough to prevent a fish being hooked. Since a normal fly can collect a leaf or two on almost every cast on the Tweed in Autumn this 'brush-off' system is a boon. A salmon will not accept a leaf-fly cocktail. It's probably this leaf-fall frustration which encourages the ignoble art of sneggling on the Tweed.

The trout angler might also be confused as whether or not to tie in a dropper. One time when fishing the Findhorn, on the next beat an angler had the misfortune to have a dropper fly go into his cheek when netting a thrashing salmon on his friend's tail fly. An alternative would be to use Balfour-Kinnear's hookless dropper-fly which seems to have gone out of fashion. He recounts this technique in his famous book, *Flying Salmon*, one of the classics.

The hookless dropper is more of a curiosity than a serious technique. I have never fished it, nor seen it fished. Nor is it a dropper in the true sense of the word. The fly, always a hackled pattern, used to be dressed on a section of wire, say half-an-inch long. This length of wire had an eye each end. The leader would be cut and the hookless fly tied into it as a link. When a fish came to this fly the angler would normally feel a 'pook' as Balfour-Kinnear described it, a small snatch or two. The angler doesn't strike until a moment later when he should feel a steady, heavy draw. The salmon has taken the first fly and as he turns with it and moves away the leader is drawn through the mouth until the tail fly comes into contact with the outside of the jaw where it gains a good hold. Whether this is legitimate fishing or deliberate foul-hooking is a matter of debate.

As the author says:

'There are three good reasons why a fish can't get rid of the casting line once it's in his mouth. First — the current is pressing it into his mouth; second, his teeth are raked back,

'I still like to fish with the great "meat hooks" of yore'.

and third, when he does open his mouth it is not to emit water, but to take it in, thereby sending the cast to the back corners of his mouth . . .'

All of this a forerunner of the present day carp-anglers' hair-rigs.

I've remarked that, after Wood, there was no new thinking about salmon fly-fishing until Reg Rhighyni investigated the relationship between changing oxygen values in the water and the taking times of salmon. I hold this to be true. Balfour-Kinnear doesn't break new ground but in his *Sheep and Shepherd* dialogue he discusses in dramatic form the various aspects of fly-fishing with more clarity than had been done before or since. The trouble is that the tempo of life today means that we have to snatch hurried fishing holidays when we can without choice of ideal conditions. The length of river we fish is likely to offer less choice of pool and we cannot flit about to choose a pool according to the direction of light or the colour of the sky. Those were more leisurely days.

I think it was Balfour-Kinnear's book which impressed on me the value of 'backing up' a pool for two reasons. There is obviously the option of showing the fly to the fish in a different way. There is also a way of overcoming a strong downstream wind by starting at the tail of the pool and casting up and across the current. The problem of the downstream wind is not so much that it makes casting difficult, but that with a floating line, it bellies downstream and makes the fly drag unmercifully. It is virtually impossible to mend line upstream to counter this.

My own contribution to the splendid armoury of salmon fly patterns is but one fly, and that not original. I have in my possession a first edition of the Francis Francis book, *Book on Angling* (1867). It became apparent to me that a particular colour had disappeared from our repertoire since Francis's day — purple. If you look through a book of modern flies you will not discover a purple salmon fly and yet it used to be a most killing colour, usually with a dash of yellow. Some patterns obtained the purple colour by blending red and blue Berlin wools, other by using plain purple mohair.

It came home to me when I was asked by the late Joe Bates Jr to contribute a chapter on Spey flies to his classic work *Atlantic Salmon Flies & Fishing*. I came across the Purple King, a typical Spey fly of that era, and another similar pattern, the 'Purpy'. Typical Spey flies were modern for their time and luckily Kelson didn't think to modify them. They were dressed on long, fine wire Dee hooks with slim bodies, long hackles from herons or Scotch cocks and with slim strips of grey or bronze mallard feather for wings. It was characteristic of these flies that the wings should be set low down on the shoulder of the hook so that together they resembled the shape of the bottom of a boat. It was also unusual insofar as one of the ribbings was wound in the reverse direction to the hackle, like a 'palmer' trout fly. I believe that the exact shade of purple for these two patterns was obtained by dyeing red Berlin wool in an infusion obtained from the moss which grows on stones, but that's by the way.

I decided to make a tube fly version of these ancient assassins. It was simple to do. A purple body silk was lapped along the tube with a narrow flat gold tinsel rib and a yellow floss-silk rib behind that, both widely spaced. The hair-wing was simply a mixture of yellow and purple bucktail. I can record that one of my acquaintances took a mighty fish of over thirty pounds with this fly on the Tweed. As this was a resurrection of the old pattern, I also resurrected that lovely old name, 'Purpy' for the fly.

I encountered another salmon fly curiosity in an old Exe and Axe pattern which I call Husband's Shrimp. I think it must be the easiest fly to dress. Many years ago, in my career as a professional fly-dresser, I was approached by an elderly angler to copy a fly he had been given when he was young by a West Country fly-tyer called Scarlet.

This fly was fashioned on a normal double iron. The body was of brown floss silk over which a red game cock hackle was palmered down the shank and secured by an oval gold ribbing. This hackle was clipped very short to give a bristle effect. The tail of the fly was formed by a large brown Spey hackle wound around the bend of the hook in the usual shrimp style. The body of this fly was given a good drenching of clear cellulose varnish until it shone. The final effect was very much like the normal brown shrimp found in the sea and it subscribes to the theory that salmon take flies which awaken their 'sea memory'.

It's curious because I have never seen any reference to the dressing in any text book, yet, clearly it must be an old traditional fly from the Axe, handed down from one generation to another.

Invariably I smile when reading meticulous instructions on how to play a fish as if the author expected you to carry his writings with you and on hooking a fish, you pull them out of your bag, saying: 'what do I do now?' There was one important discovery made by Alexander Wanless, a prolific writer of pre-war days who tried to popularise what was then known as 'threadline' fishing. Briefly, this consisted of fishing a fly with an ultra-light spinning rod and fixed-spool reel. Casting weight was obtained by using a strip of plastic material which Wanless called a 'controller'. The method died out, giving way to its cruder offspring, bubble-float fishing.

The early models of fixed-spool reel were only capable of casting very fine lines, hence the term 'threadline'.

Wanless became unpopular because he killed an immense number of huge sea trout and salmon with lines of just a couple of pounds breaking strain. He discovered that fish fought pressure. If that pressure is relieved by opening the pick-up of the reel, then the salmon would quietly return to its lie, unaware that it was attached to a line by a hook. On hooking a big fish on his threadline outfit, Wanless would immediately release the pressure, the fish would lie quietly whilst Wanless got well below. Then, by gently easing its head round so that water entered behind the gill covers, Wanless successfully 'drowned' his quarry. I have profited from this strange behaviour on occasion with many species of fish, and I described it in my book *Big Pike*. Recollecting this, Clive Loveland hooked a monster pike in Belvoir lake, just a few ounces short of the then record. He immediately eased off the pressure and gently coaxed the hooked fish into his net.

I well remember that I faced my first salmon fishing expedition with trepidation. I could not afford a private beat with a gillie who, legend had it, needed to be plied with single malts and slices of cold game-pie. The first problem was the simplest. Where were the fish? Salmon leap, don't they? That's what the word 'Salar' means in the Latin tongue, the leaper. They do not always leap from the place in which they lie. A salmon may move several feet before it leaves the water, and, on returning to the river, it drops back again into that lie. Again, the books tell of the 'lie' as if that were the resting place of the fish, and then I watched bemused when a Dee salmon moved continually in a wide circle in the pool, jumping here, jumping there.

The classic lie, the book told me, was five feet of water over a flat ledge of rock. Why, then, did the angler in front of me fish down a shallowish run on the North Esk, and take a fish from it? And the great whorl in the salmon run reflected a rock which was submerged several feet above in the fast current. It was very confusing.

Ah yes, how much easier to have broken out the piggy bank and hired that beat with a gillie to call one 'sir', to tie on the right fly and place one in the right casting place for a particular lie? And then the friendly local angler would leave the water, sit down by one's side and point out where the fish would be at normal height, and where they would rest in high water. He would advise on favourite fly patterns, and the size of fly to choose at a particular height of water. He habitually took a hundred fish out of this river each year. Slowly the confidence builds.

Then, gillie-less, you go to other fishings. You know how to read the water. You take its temperature to decide whether to fish sinking or floating line. You have a feeling where the fish will lie. It gradually dawns on you that salmon fly-fishing is a purely mechanical business, that at some mysterious conjunction of light, temperature and dissolved oxygen the fish will be in a taking mood, so that if your fly comes above his eyes at that time, the fish will follow and take. You get into the right routine, the swing of it, you keep at it, the fish takes.

The classic book on salmon fishing has pictures of equally classical pools, and each one will be marked with a little cross to show you where the fish will be lying. The text will describe these places, will tell you that the fish wants it this way or that, with a safe amount of water above its head, a nice safe and deep area to run into if pursued by an otter. The problem is that the visiting fish accepts the river as he finds it, for it has run this same river instinctively for thousands of years, much as Captain Ahab explained to Starbuck, that it had all been foretold a million years before that ocean rolled. In heavy water the fish will run through slacks and close to banks. In low water the fish will pass through shallow runs because it must. It will rest in those places if it has to.

Salmon lying on landing net

I do not find it astonishing that lady anglers figure so prominently in the lists of the biggest salmon caught on fly. I have explained that salmon fishing is purely mechanical and women are said to be the most practical of people.

On being invited to allow my name to go forward for membership of the Fly Fishers Club, knowing the answer, and reminding myself of those words of Groucho Marx, 'Why should I spend good money to join clubs which lets in people like me?' I murmured that I would be pleased to have a London watering hole where I could take my wife and dog. 'Oh no!' riposted the horrified misogynist. 'We don't allow women . . . might stretch a point for the dog.'

Having met a goodly number of expert anglers of the majority sex, I declined to let my name go forward for the blackball.

The serious point is that fly-fishing for salmon is a practical matter, the management of the line so that it brings the fly to the fish in such a way that it comes into the fish's vision naturally, neither whipping round too quickly, nor sinking sullenly. The fly rod, properly managed, does this more efficiently than the spinning rod.

You know, there's not much more to it than that.

Chapter 14
Beck and Call

'Je crois que je n'ai jamais pêché avec une mouche portant un nom anglais. Je sais bien que les mouches anglaises ont été conçues par de vrais pêcheurs et que leur efficacité est éprovée. Mais si je pêche avec un Blue Winged Olive ou une Hare's Ear, je ne me sens pas à l'aise. J'ai le sentiment d'être un peu ridicule quand j'essaie de prononcer ces termes avec mon accent franc-comtois.'

Repertoire des Mouches Artificielles Françaises*
Jean-Paul Pequegnot

The River Traun was a favourite fishing place of Charles Ritz. The trouble is that when you fish in Austria, like the losers at Yorktown, you're inclined to sing that the World has been turned topsy-turvy. For one thing Austrian fly-fishers much prefer to catch and eat grayling than trout, an attitude which reduced many a Test purist to apoplexy. Then there's the tackle. The Austrian angler loves a very short stiff rod, and for preference he loads it with a cheap line, not to save money, but because it is stiffer than the top quality product.

When you see his river, all becomes clear! The Alm, which I fished, is a tributary of the mighty Traun, and it crashes down from its mountain heights with the force of a runaway locomotive. You

---

*I believe that I have never fished using a fly with an English name. I know full well that English flies were created by true fishermen and that they have been proven very effective. But if I fish with a Blue Winged Olive or a Hare's Ear I never feel at ease. I feel somewhat foolish when I try to pronounce these names with my local accent.

step into the river, and, facing upstream, the battering of the current takes your breath away. If you're not wearing thermal waders the ice-cold water from the melting snows of the peaks pierces your flesh to the very bone. It's scarcely possible to throw a line upstream, so down and across is the golden rule, even for dry fly, whilst the shattering force of the river pummelling your back tries to overturn you. The footing is precarious, for glassy slides of chalk lie between the pebble runs.

You have fishery management taken very seriously in Austria. My friend, Manfred, although a member of the syndicate, was only allocated eleven days a season on this stretch of the river. I was ushered up the worn staircase of the monastery, which administers the fishery, and there the kindly Franciscan peered into my eyes to identify the colour to enter into the passport-like fishing permit. Then we went to the river.

Being an old hand on Tees and Derwent I thought I was used to fishing fast water, but the Alm was something else. The short rod, say of only seven feet, took some getting used to, for it had the lightning-stiff action of a coarse fisher's ledgering tool. Manfred had given me a bushy sedge fly with a closely wound palmer hackle of grizzle cock. The trick was to wade down the middle of the Alm, flicking the fly into tiny pockets of quieter water at the very edges of the river. As luck would have it, this was just a day or two after the close of the brown trout season, and although grayling were the target, the brownies kept coming to the fly.

I soon came to appreciate the Austrian's love of grayling when I hooked my first lady-of-the-stream which hectored my rod like a virago! The fish erects its great sailfin in that pounding current and the pressure is shattering. It was curious, too, to fish high in the mountain country, with golden sunlight as if in mid-summer, yet with odd flurries of snow reminding me just where I was.

Was it not Wellington, at Waterloo, who said, 'Hard pounding, Gentlemen,' after having had a few 'whiffs of grapeshot' from the French cannon? I know how he felt! I emerged from the Alm with my joints feeling as if Torquemada had been asking me a few simple questions whilst on the rack. The Austrian anglers have the answer to this, for many a small town has its municipal baths where a ram-jet of water massages you whilst you cling for dear life to a safety bar in its jet.

Then they said we must visit Herr Brunner, the famous rod maker of Steyr who fashioned in split cane those wicked little rods which dominate Traun and Alm.

'Of course, I can make one for you,' he promised. 'I have a few customers waiting, but I should get it to you in two years time!' It sounded like the promise of a Moscow plumber being called to a burst pipe, so I reluctantly declined. So back to my motel by the side of the vast Danube, where I was the only resident to be lulled to sleep by the mournful hootings of the steamers as they slid by like ghosts in the river mists.

Monsieur Faudemer was a genuine hero of the French resistance. A bizarre coincidence linked his courage to my cowardice, for the very house in which his 'controller' lived, during the war, was later the surgery of my dentist! The Gestapo cottoned on to my old friend, but he managed to escape before they came for him. He then had to hide in the forests and fields of Normandy until the liberation came. It was one of the many recognitions he was given, to be appointed President of the local APP, which is a semi-official angling preservation society which each area has in France.

He owned a stretch of a trout stream called the River Eaulne. This stream was, in its turn, a tributary of the Arques. It is paradoxical to see this peaceful valley where Henry of Navarre won a bloody victory over the army of the Duke of Mayenne, for local anglers were startled to find themselves fighting even stranger battles in the river. A local experimenter tipped some Pacific salmon parr into the Arques system, and to everyone's consternation, over the next few years giant hump-backs were running up the tributaries. Authority was not amused; the offender was fined heavily.

My last visit to M. Faudemer and his stream was a celebration of sparking white table linen and equally sparkling ice-cold champagne, served on the lawn of his bungalow which stood on a little hill, overlooking the stream and its quaint fishing hut with heron weathercock.

I always feel at home in France, for if you shook my mother's family tree several Gallic ancestors would fall out, and besides being brought up to be bi-lingual, I'm afraid that at some very early age 'vin ordinaire' must have replaced cow's milk. I was yet astonished when the local fly fishermen divided the natural insects of the river into two categories, the important mayflies and the rest, insignificant small flies dismissively called 'moucherons'. Not for them the subtle distinctions between olives, sedges and spinners. They were all 'moucherons'.

The banks of the stream were in those days neglected and tree-lined save where the course passed through a working farmyard.

There, one day, a comfortable old sow was flank-deep in the water, keeping cool in the sultry weather, and a tempting trout was rising steadily between herself and the bank. I took this fish on a Pont-Audemer, the favoured copy of the mayfly in that part of Normandy.

This fly is a curiosity because, although it's highly appreciated by fish and fisherman alike in Normandy, it is closely related to an old English pattern, the Mole Fly, which has fallen into disuse, even on the River Mole where it was invented and from which it takes its name. Even more curious, so popular is the Mole Fly format in France that many popular variations are in constant use, amongst them being 'la Président Billard, la Pont-l'Eveque, l'Ermenault, la Grisette, la Catillon' — they all descend from the humble Mole Fly. The important thing about the Pont-Audemer is that it is properly fished in an unusual posture, with its body and tail pointing downwards through the surface film whilst the fly is supported on the surface film by its collar of hackle fibres. It's dressing comes from that orthodox mayfly stable which used raffia in its natural state for the body, ribbed with a strand of bronze peacock herl. The legs are a simple Rhode Island Red cock hackle, and wings, sloping forward over the eye of the hook, are made from a tuft of silver mallard flank feather.

My companions didn't differentiate between dun and spinner artificials during the entire mayfly season, which, on the Eaulne was prolific. The Pont-Audemer succeeded throughout the hatch of duns and fall of spinners. I managed to take fish with the spent black drake patterns described elsewhere. When the mayfly was over, then my friends lost interest in the fly, it was the time for those damned 'moucherons'.

A local favourite fly was a variation of Pont-Audemer — and there are many of them. This one boasted a stripped hackle stalk for the body, the Lunn school of thought. An intelligent tactic they employed was to dress the mayfly copies on normal dry fly hooks,

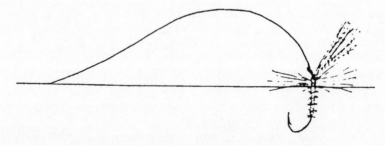

The posture of the Pont-Audemer on the water.

and not the long-shanked ones which we are wedded to here. It's strange, that fishing on the Test with John Goddard, he tied his mayflies on the same sized hooks as my friends in Normandy, and he did great work with them. I like to fish with the orthodox monsters. Why? Just because they are so handsome in box and on water alike.

It was pleasant to come back to the home of M. Faudemer. He was incensed. He had read a newspaper article published in London in which it referred to the Battle of Hastings being won by William the Conqueror and his 'French army'.

'You tell him, when you get back, that it was not a French army. It was Norman.' By then we were drinking the local cider, so how could I refuse?

⚜

From cider to wine, for the River Vin means simply that. It is an almost unfished little trout stream which flows into the mighty Atrann, near to Fauconberg, in Southern Sweden. Although it held, and still holds nice trout, the banks are lined by Elder trees which harbour a fly of the same name. These trout gorge themselves on the green Elder fly, so much so that their own flesh becomes ghostly-green in colour and bitter to the tongue. With scorching hot weather, my friend Görann and I could only stand the heat between four and six in the morning. All you had to do was to dress and fish the dry green-fly. And return the fish!

The Atrann, that is a salmon river. I was introduced to it by the skilled Swedish fly-tyer, Margrethe Thomson who owned a stretch. Another stream, a virtual cataract fell from a mill above into the river, and local historians claim that Vikings built their boats in the forest then winched them down the waterfall into the Atrann below. Margrethe was of Danish origin, and she loved to recount the story of a wartime visit by the German Governor of Norway, General Falkenhorst who was being shown around the museum in Oslo. He expressed some surprise at the modest size of the Viking longboats.

'But at least we did get to England in these boats,' the Curator pointed out.

Margrethe tied for me the Red Sandy, the pattern she swore by for the Atrann. This is an old Scottish fly, probably from the Halladale, and it gave some forward promise of the later success of the General Practitioner. Nowadays we would need to simplify Kelson's old dressing, for the Indian Crow and Jungle Cock feathers come from protected birds.

Frank Sawyer had rewards when he fished his Grey Goose nymphs on the forest lakes in Central Sweden. They told me about it, then went on fishing their beloved Woolly Worms which can be made from virtually any colour combination of materials which take the fancy, of a chenille body along a long-shanked lure hook, matching or contrasting hackle held down with a tinsel rib. My last evening in the woodland near to Jønkoping, a fire breaking out on the far bank, then loud, tuneless singing with gales of laughter.

'It's that Russian party from the Embassy,' they told me. 'They fish until dark, get drunk on vodka, light a fire to cook the fish, sing sad Slavonic songs and eventually fall asleep.' The reflection of the fire shone on the surface of the lake. In the middle of the blood-red water spread the ripples of a rising fish.

France and Britain share a wide diversity of landscape and of fishing conditions. I was called to a famous hook-making firm in Eastern France to help design fly hooks. I longed to escape from the flat lands between the two mountain ranges, the 'trou de Belfort', through which invading armies have traditionally stormed in troublous times. My companions there were shooting fanatics. I was not, so it fell to my lot at week-ends to join the teams of beaters who hallooed, blew small trumpets and clapped their hands whilst walking abreast through the forest to drive the chevreuil and sanglier towards the line of guns.

I would lift my eyes to the distant shadows of the Jura mountains.

'Surely,' I asked Norbert, 'there must be a grayling stream up there?' For this was November when the trumpet fanfares echoed through the villages of Franche-Comté to commemorate the fallen of the two great wars.

'I'm fed up with shooting, too. We only hit one skunk this morning. I'll take you to the Dessoubre. We should get some grayling there.'

So, the following Saturday saw us wending our way up into the Jura mountains, the river tumbling downhill by the roadside. We stopped in the mountain village of Sainte Hippolyte to collect local flies.

'What we need for this river,' exclaimed Norbert 'is the local favourite, le Mauve.'

This was the only place where I had encountered the beautifully dressed tiny dry-flies from the hands of Madame de Chamberet. They were made on size 16 and 18 hooks with steely-pointed hackles of unusual colours, violet, dark green, and pink. I collected a pattern which took my eye. It had a body of bright red quill, a violet hackle and tail fibres of cream cock.

Leaving the village behind, we followed the course of the River Dessoubre until we came to a place where a chute of rock blocked further progress, and rumblings in the mountains above warned that blasting was in progress, hence the rockfall.

A late Autumn sun lit up the shallows of the river as I started to fish 'uphill'. The stream didn't fall with the tumultuous panache of the Alm. There were pleasant glides behind jutting rock-corners where grayling would bring that distinctive bubble, as they shot from the bottom to pick off an insect from behind the place in which they lay. The miniscule 'Mauve' fly did great execution, but, even so, a visitor from Britain finds the democratic local habit of throwing flies to great distances with bubble float and fixed spool reel, somewhat disconcerting.

After a few hours rockhopping, we stretched our aching legs on a grassy ledge whilst my friend told me of his local-fly preferences. One of these has come across the Channel to us, the Cul de Canard. I have long resented the taste which fly-inventors have for disgusting materials. R. S. Austin of Tiverton* regarded it as indispensable for his followers to pursue infuriated rams around a ten acre field in order to purloin some dubbing fur from their scrotums! I denied myself the pleasure of this harvest having seen the havoc wreaked on a shiny car panel by a jealous Swaledale tup who took his own reflection for a rival for the favours of his favourite ewe. On returning from his fruitless day on Selset reservoir, and surveying the wreckage, the victim asked the bailiff if the Water Authority would pay for the damage.

'No. You should have a muddy old Land-Rover, like mine' was the unsympathetic response.

Now, I was told, there was a particular feather right by the stern orifice of a wild duck which was waterproofed by a certain gland, and this would make an unsinkable fly! This fly, the 'Cul de Canard' as fished in the Franche-Comté, was made with a body of yellow tying silk, a light blue dun cock hackle with the duck's self-lubricating feather in front.

It is agreeable to find in the Jura region flies which are peculiar to single villages as used to be the case generations ago in Hampshire. Then there was the Whitchurch Dun, the Kimbridge Killer, and so on. One of these patterns took my fancy. It is the Jean-Marie which, quite independently, solved the same problem

*Famous as the inventor, in the early years of this Century, of Tup's Indispensable.

143

which Canon Greenwell faced so many years ago. And it solved this problem in the same way, with the added virtue that whereas the Greenwell was targetted on olive duns, the Jean-Marie is favoured for duns and spinners alike. The hackled dry-fly has rust-coloured tail whisks, yellow tying-thread body and a medium blue dun cock hackle wound in front of a natural red one. The fly has proved an excellent ambassador on Border rivers like the Teviot, always used as a floater.

It's my opinion that, although each country, and even rivers and locations, grew their own fly traditions which we uncover by research, they have common origins which are revealed more by linguistic clues than angling history. Many fly-tyers now believe that a good proportion of our native patterns hailed once from Ireland. Jean-Paul Pequegnot, in his book quoted at the head of this section, tells of a fly from the bocage of Brittany, called the Ruz-Du. 'Ruz' is the word for 'red' in the Breton dialect. 'Du' signifies black in the same tongue, and, coincidentally, Lesley Crawford gives a list of common Gaelic names for lochs in the excellent guide she produced to the lakes in Caithness and Sutherland. She tells us that Loch Dubh means black loch. In the old Breton tongue 'coch' meant 'red' and how does that relate to the Welsh 'Coch-y-bondhu' fly? The conundrum is this: did the fly travel and take the words, or did the words travel and take the flies? You tell me.

It is true that when we try to find the exact material for a certain pattern of fly we do not realise that what we are seeking is something which the inventor was easily able to lay his hands on, and that convenience is the way in which many famous flies were born. In the golden days of Empire there was considerable social stratification in fishing and the ghost of this snobbery haunts us just a little today. Reading back through the history of fly-fishing, sprinklings of generals and admirals crop up where ever salmon fishing is discussed. It is easy to understand how fly patterns with complex wings evolved out of the plumages which soldiers found in the Zulu and Ashanti wars.

Later more practical patterns came from the less exotic places in which the army found itself. In that nasty little skirmish in Mesopotamia the rankers found themselves latching on to the giant Euphrates 'salmon' using offal as bait, the gamier the better. These fish, caught in both the Tigris and Euphrates, were very much like the Indian Mahseer which some of the soldiers had already met when quelling Sepoy mutinies in earlier times. The Mahseer, though, had such large scales that they were cleaned and dried and pressed into service for playing cards and ash-trays. The Mahseer fishing became an integral part of life in India, so much so that Hardy Bros were regularly visited by young officers receiving their first posting to the land of 'John Company'. Hardy made a special range of tackle for the Mahseer, to be bought and packed away with the pig-sticking outfit. Of course, the red-tabbed staff-officer wouldn't be seen dead affixing lumps of rotting meat to hurl into the Tigris, so he needs must have his salmon fly rod sent out to 'Messpot'.

Then the flies had to be made from the odds and ends lying around the cantonment, and before long Major-General H. T. Brooking was writing home to announce that his colleague Brigadier-General Dunsford had invented a fly which was a certain killer of the 'Tigris salmon'. Dressed on a size 1/0 iron, the tail was the pointed feather from a local sand grouse, the body was made from a fibre of material taken from coconut matting, ribbed with a silver strip cut from the lining of a packet of Capstan cigarettes. A discarded shaving brush provided the badger hair for the throat hackle and the wings were taken from the black and white spotted feathers from a black partridge. The fly was duly named the 'Capstan' and accounted for fish up to 12lb. The big specimens, running up to 80lb or more, remained true to their plebeian taste and hurled themselves at the privates' rotting meat-bait, and the Capstan fly sank into the desert sands, its name forgotten until now . . . although I came across a similar bass fly from Alabama called the 'Hopsack' the body of which was similarly fashioned from what was lying around at the time. The war against the 'Tigris Salmon' took hold of the public imagination and in 1917, the *Morning Post* was collecting tackle from London tackle shops to send out to the troops as part of the 'Mesopotamia Comforts Fund'.

This curiosity demonstrates how flies were invented, and to this day it's a foolish person who buys an 'olive dun' carpet for the house of a keen angler, whilst dogs named 'Garry' and 'Tosh' had bald patches which testified to the sporting instincts of fishing parsons! The Welsh Collie also passed on its name to that strange salmon fly which has little but a four inch length of curly hair to act like the old-fashioned eel-tail bait, and, by being stripped through the water to excite salmon, it revives again that long forgotten dodge of 'pulling-off' which that well-known pre-war salmon fisherman Balfour-Kinnear used to bestir a 'stiff' salmon.

I was amused to read that there was once a time when users of horsehair lines and leaders were sceptical about the virtues of the new-fangled silk-worm gut. In the year eighteen-hundred, 'North Country Angler' was a snapper-up of unconsidered trifles and he tells us:

> 'I saw, in London, a large dappled grey horse which, I was told, the owner, a brewer, valued at one hundred and fifty guineas. I consulted with my landlord, who dealt largely with him, how to get some hairs from his tail, which was the finest and longest I ever saw. The drayman loved a drink. A bribe will do wonders. I had above two hundred brought for me for two shillings and a pot of beer; I would not have taken sixpence for the worst of them.'

'North Country Angler' also had a practical way of restocking his dubbing bag. He continues:

> 'I met with a beggar once at Durham, that had a strong curled beard. I persuaded him to let me get it cut off, or shaved dry. That furnished me with excellent dubbing for salmon and large fish, and because I had been kind to him, he brought me soon after a great quantity of a more shining yellow. Some of these hairs I mixed with soft swine's down, or other dubbing, for almost every fly I dressed. And I made them resemble the whisks and feet of flies to a great nicety.'

So, Skues' method of mixing dubbing furs to obtain special effects was known at least a century before.

The memory of Skues came to me when I was fishing that milky little chalk stream, the Simistid, in Denmark, This stream is quite small, and I was a guest of the genial Danish fly-tyer, Prebend Torp Jacobsen who forged through the rising corn like a galleon in full sail in his anxiety to reach the river. Simistid fish are spooky because nowhere is the river deep. Before long my mind was thrown back to the furious debates which Skues launched around the turn of the Century. He enraged the British rod-making hierarchy simply by accusing them of making rods which were far too heavy, and he brought his own rods in from the American firm of Leonard. To prove his point, the Leonard rods, even in those days of split cane, were only of a few ounces, where here they were preaching the virtues of steel-centres and double-building.

I have avoided tackle discussions because invention overtakes obsolescence on winged feet, but this is an age-old duel which had a bearing on my own thinking, and was brought painfully home to me by a severe attack of tennis elbow. Next time my Danish friends were putting the Schnapps into the freezer to celebrate our victories on the Simistid, Guden and Haltum rivers, I was using a rod to my own design which threw an AFTM size 2 double-taper line.

A succession of dry summers brought water levels so low in Britain that I rediscovered my light-line thrower, to cast very small flies to spooky fish in low, clear lakes and streams. I christened the rod the 'Brightwater', and had a blank-maker produce the rod-tubes for me in lengths from 7 to 10 feet. Only later did it dawn on me that it was probably the first time a rod-series was made in half a dozen lengths for the same two lines, sizes DT 2 & 3. My friend, the British International Fly Team competitor, Colin North, inveigled the ten-footer from me, and progressing down the Teviot before me, he was taking sea trout visitors, one after another.

'Can I have my rod back?' I asked, plaintively.

'Well, not really', he replied.

My Danish friends introduced me to that strange fly they called the 'Flymph'. It was not quite an 'emerger'. It copied the stage just before the adult dun emerged from its nymphal shuck, when the nymph was in the surface film, but, as yet, unhatched. It was, in effect, a floating nymph. Dressing the Flymph is simplicity itself once it is known what species of fly it has to copy, for it can be made to attack fish feeding on any dun at the surface, iron blue, medium olive, pale watery and, at a pinch, stonefly or sedge. The style is the same. It consists of a body dubbing with tail fibres to match, and a hen hackle wound sparsely at the head, sloping backwards.

My old friend, the Pale Evening Dun speckled the evening Simistid, and the Flymph version proved as good an executioner as Jack Ketch on a busy day at Tyeburn. The body was of pale cream dubbing with a mere soupçon of scarlet fibres blended in. The tail and throat hackle was of pale honey dun. That's all. It's funny how some good American flies nip over into Scandinavia, passing us by in Britain, and V. S. Hidy's remarkably intelligent Flymph is one of these.

Undoubtedly I would have supported the great campaigns of Skues, for lighter rods, for sensible nymph fishing, for trying to keep the spirit of 'native wildness' in the chalk streams. Although I can't be certain, I have a feeling that I wouldn't have chosen him as a fishing companion, for in his writing he comes across as an expert who had a competitive impatience, especially with the less gifted, who, on failing to rise a fish were enjoined to 'move over and let me have a chuck . . .' and inevitably, in the language of the time, the novice would 'have his eye wiped' by the 'crack hand'; on one of those 'halcyon days', I suppose.

If you skim through a scientific tome on the fauna and flora of the aquatic environment, say Macan and Worthington's excellent *Life in Lakes and Rivers*, you discover a rough and ready way of classifying rivers. The higher section, sometimes in mountainous terrain is where the rain-fed current is powerful enough to move stones and pebbles and break them down into gravel. In these upper reaches the water temperature is usually cool, as poets testify. Trout and Miller's Thumb are the fishy inhabitants, though as the stream reaches the foothills and its slower current allows small areas of silt to collect, then minnows are at home there. The food-life is sparse, nutrients are scarce and the hard-working trout are mostly small as a consequence. Once in a while some great cannibal trout astonishes us. A seven pound brute was found jammed in the grill of a grating at Langdon Beck after a flood. These are rare surviviors which have switched to a fish-only diet. They have heads like bull terriers.

Of course, Nature doesn't require fish to grow large. It only requires them to survive and reproduce. When I was a young fly fisher I was the proud possessor of a book by an angler called Clapham who delighted in stalking the moorland becks in plus-fours, expertly to winkle out the sharp little trout which lived there. It was in a time when Parental Authority didn't mind if village lads learned their angling craft with the top section of an old lancewood rod loaded with a length of well-soaked flax cuttyhunk sea line. This would throw a fly or creeper far enough upstream to tempt the moorland fish. The art of fly-fishing was mastered on bloody knees.

Clapham didn't mind how he fished, and this was right given a sparse fishery which no one else wanted to fish, save these younger lads. He would livebait with minnow, fish the creeper and worm and go upstream with the fly. When the stream was too thin for his sectioned rod, he would ditch the lower pieces, push the reel into his pocket and whip away with the top piece only.

It's axiomatic that fly life diminishes as you move into higher reaches of streams. It breeds the false belief that fish will be so hungry that they will snatch at anything, but that is wrong. Trout can be capricious everywhere and even fisheries which have a reputation for dour trout testify to the fact that we do not understand their feeding behaviour in that place. Emotional moods do not come into it. The range of fly life being restricted does mean that a modest range of patterns can be used on moorland becks. Whereas Clapham would have preferred the Stewart spider patterns, with the occasional Spanish needle for the stonefly, my early choice was to tie a weighted pheasant tail nymph on the point

'. . . in these upper reaches the water is usually cool'.

with a dry grey duster about eighteen inches above. The pheasant tail is an excellent copy of small stonefly larvae.

The rest is common sense. Trout must lie in secret places, holes beneath undercut banks, in the deep, dark places where the current is stayed by an obstacle, in small weirs. Some of Clapham's love of the moorland becks rubbed off on me, so that I determined to try my hand at them when I first had the opportunity. The upper reaches of the Whiteadder, and its tributary, the Dye brought home to me the point which Clapham made insistently, that it is wrong to wed oneself to tiny flies simply because the beck and the fish are small. Although the fly life from the water itself is limited in range, the fish come to rely on terrestrial insects carried by the wind, heather flies and moths, beetles and so on.

A problem which Skues solved for me was how to keep a fly buoyant on the little knotty whorls and ripples of tumbling streams. I dislike clipping-short hackles, but orthodox dry-flies drown quickly. Skues once described the trick of untwisting the tying thread, keeping it open with a needle, then laying in a row of hair which can be wound as a hackle. It was an ancient formula for the Hare's Ear and it makes the most efficient collar which can be left at normal hackle length, or clipped short for the hatching nymph. With care it may also be wound around a short hackle-stalk butt to form a hair-hackle parachute fly.

So, when scrambling uphill in the footsteps of Clapham, eventually I came to rely solely on a two-fly leader. The point was a slightly loaded hare's ear nymph, dressed in the two-tone style described earlier. About eighteen inches above, on a shortish dropper, I tied on the dry-fly version with hackle-hair collar, both to act as a sight-bob and to take fish in its own right.

It's plain common sense to fish these becks 'upstream'. These streams are so low and clear without rain that it is impossible to approach trout from above without spooking them. That old favourite cast, 'the cross country', which used to be described in Clapham's 'Roaring Twenties', but never today, is a useful tactic to put distance between caster and fly. It simply means laying a good part of the fly line across intervening land, and this is usually a spiteful place of sharp stones. It makes good sense to reserve an old, worn line for that purpose. The 'cross country' cast also allows you to stalk fish from the softer, noise-free margins of the beck.

There are things which are so obvious that I feel like the egg-sucking expert instructing Grandma. Yet I once invited a friend to accompany me on a beck-fishing foray into the Lammermuir Hills, and he turned up with all of his southern reservoir gear, heavy waders, huge net, bulging bag, the lot. After half-a-mile of rock-hopping he would have been exhausted. Even Mr Clapham crammed everything into a wickerwork creel and mostly clambered uphill in his plus-fours and brogues. His stockings would dry out quickly in such hot work. I never encumbered myself with a net, and the modern fly-fisher's vest is a boon. If you have more than you can fit into its pockets, you're carrying too much for moorland becks and hill lochs alike.

It's equally foolish to dismiss the moorland trout as of too little account compared, say to a fat Southern rainbow stockie. Clapham's slim volume conveyed to me years ago his love of the wild, open expanses of lonely moorland with its wheeling buzzards and startled grouse. And fishing those becks is like going back to school. The casting has to be accurate, the stalking like Geronimo and striking like Mercury.

I see that my line has almost run down to the spool. This book has sought to bring together the strands of my fly-fishing philosophy. The first of these is a trust in the faithful traditions. I have eschewed the invention of new fly patterns merely to satisfy the 'flavour of the month' appetite, though where I have found a gap unfilled, as in the early failure to find an adequate copy of the buzzer pupa, then I have endeavoured to fill it, as with my Footballer fly.

The second endeavour has been to become an all-round fly fisher who could turn his rod to any species and any technique in any part of this land, and further abroad. The drive of this book has been to prove that one can overcome the 'jack of all trades, master of none' syndrome when a new, unknown water is first encountered.

And, lastly, I hope the book reflects another strand of my philosophy, that anglers should help and teach each other, encouraging newcomers and novices to improve their skills, even if it means avoiding the competitive element which is creeping into our sport.

Into these three strands I have tried to weave the historical fabric of fly-fishing, picking out those great iconoclasts from the past whose thinking changed the way we fish.

As I write these lines one of our leading thinkers predicts a doomsday scenario. He says that civilisation has only fifty years to run before it will be overwhelmed by catastrophes which are in the pipeline, one of which is the snowballing degradation of the environment. It is this threat to the quality and volume of waters flowing through our river banks which concerns us. There are grounds for pessimism. I have felt dismayed by the apathy shewn by bureaucrats and their political masters when I have campaigned for a vaccine for Weil's disease, for example.

It is a time for choices. It is a time when we hope Authority will no longer regard a grand river like the Tees as a carrier to dispose of unwanted poisons to be dispersed into the oceans. There is still time to make the wise choices — just! That dreadful phrase, 'short termism' expresses the fear that one day migratory fish will no longer be able to run the poison barriers in the North Sea. I am not as pessimistic as our prophets of doom. I think it could go either way. I do believe that politicians only act on environmental dangers when public opinion forces them to do so. That means, if we care enough, we have to support our national and international bodies which have already achieved a great deal in buying off estuarine salmon nets. The inevitable, and final question is: do we care enough? Only time will tell.

Cul de Canard feathers

Appendix
Special Fly Patterns

❧

God made bees and bees made honey.
God made men and men made money,
But the Devil, he made lawyers and 'torneys,
And placed them in Ulverston and Broughton-
    in-Furness'

Lines from an old Lakeland poem.

From the time of the popular angling press, say from 1880 onwards, it was always possible to trace the originator of a fly, and its correct dressing. For example, when some doubts were cast on the parentage of the Greenwell, the innovative Canon was able to give chapter and verse in the *Fishing Gazette*. We have seen that George Kelson was, for a while, able to hijack other peoples' inventions from an earlier time when records were sketchy. I decided to trace a fly from those earlier times, the Broughton Point. I mention this fly because it was rediscovered by two friends who used it to great effect in Upper Teesdale. Although the fly is not widely known they found examples of it in local tackle shops.

There was a vague belief that the fly was a still-water pattern, first used on Ullswater, and that it owed its name to Broughton-in-Furness.

This was wrong. The fly was invented by a shoemaker from Penrith, probably around 1840, and his name was Jack Broughton. His favourite haunts were the Eden and Eamont. The fly was a successful copy of the Iron Blue Dun. You may imagine that anglers he encountered on the river bank cadged samples from him so that by the end of the century it was so popular that most fly-tying houses offered it in their catalogues. Confusion reigned because in Jack Broughton's time record-keeping was scanty, and he left no written account.

Tracking down nineteenth century dressers, we have Hutchinson's catalogue of country flies giving a body of purple silk, hackle of bright starling with dun coloured fur at the shoulder and wings from the starling primary quills. The famous fly-maker from Hawes, James Blade, agreed body colour and wing but preferred a black hen hackle with a morsel of bright red in front. William Baigent, however, chose a dark mulberry silk body whilst a Carlisle tyer, Strong, went for light purple. Niven and Edmonds thought the body should be purple but John Jackson tied the body with red-brown silk. The famous Michael Theakston insisted the body should be well-waxed orange silk whereas Mrs Knight, a well-supported fly-tyer in Penrith used a tasteful sky-blue silk.

My own philosophy has been to rely on traditional patterns in my fishing life. I have only gone in for inventions when I perceived there to be a positive gap which I needed to fill to kill fish, hence the Footballer, which, I believe may well have been the first properly imitative copy of the buzzer pupa. And within the orthodox structure of traditional fly styling, I have sought modestly to improve fish-taking qualities of the fly. I have tried to avoid the 'flavour of the month' syndrome, though I've never denied the pleasure which amateur fly-tyers enjoy from inventing new patterns even if most of them do not stay the course . . . after all, the only real critic is the fish.

I have grouped together the flies I have used according to their type, and not by the book's sections. I have not repeated standard dressings of popular flies which are in all text books, but I list rarer patterns, innovations and variations which, I hope will add to your angling success.

Dry Flies

The patterns described are also intended as additions and variations on standard patterns.

DADDY LONGLEGS
Hook	— size 10 standard dry-fly
Body	— plastic mayfly body
Legs	— six strands of Golden Pheasant tail, knotted, and tied three on each side on the hook in front of the body, and secured by figure-of-eight turns of thread
Hackles	— two Cree cock hackles, tied in at their butts and wound towards eye. The points are separated and tied 'spent' to form the wings

A longer pattern can be made with the same wings, legs and hackles structure but substituting brown goose herl, ribbed with gold wire on a long-shanked mayfly hook

DAMSEL FLY
Hook	— long shanked mayfly, size 8 or 10
Body	— blue lurex, ribbed black button-thread
Wings	— either grizzle cock hackle points, or grey partridge hackles, tied 'spent'
Hackle	— grizzle cock
Head	— black ostrich or bronze peacock herl

GINGER QUILL (Pale Watery Dun)
Hook	— size 12-14 standard dry-fly or preferably a wide gape grub-hook
Tail	— a hefty bunch of cock fibres, ginger, tied down the hook bend to reach the water-surface
Body	— bronze peacock herl, stripped, and wound as to expose the white root at the tail of the fly
Hackles	— 1. Ginger cock, tied normally, 2. Pale blue wound back-to-front to splay legs, porcupine style

Note: this pattern may be repeated in style for many dry-flies, with two aims, to splay the hackles and to obtain two-tone contrasting colours in the body and legs.

LECKFORD PROFESSOR (Cow's Arse)
Hook	— sizes 12-16 dry-fly or wide-gape grub hook
Hackles	— 1. red game cock

                   2. white cock
                   these are tightly wound at the hook bend
Body   — rabbit or hare body fur, ribbed fine silver round
                   tinsel.

This fly is designed to fish fast water, and may be cast onto the bankside vegetation, to be twitched off to assault fish lying tight to the bank.

MARCH BROWN (Fast Water version)
Hook   — size 12 dry-fly
Tail   — fibres of brown partridge hackle
Body   — finely cut strip of brown underbark from the
                   silver birch tree, ribbed brown thread
Hackles   — stiff white cock in front of which are two brown
                   partridge hackles.

Note: the underbark, which is found by first removing the top silver bark, is a corky type material with superb buoyancy, and was used in the 19th Century. There's also a buff-cream underbark which makes excellent mayfly bodies, similarly ribbed.

HOOLET (Brown Moth Wake-Fly)
Hook   — sizes 6 and 8 standard dry-fly
Body   — twisted strands of bronze peacock herl, wound to
                   make a plump, fuzzy body over a sliver of cork
                   lashed to underside of hook shank
Wing   — any browny speckled feather slip, tied flat, and
                   rolled over hook shank to split the wing.
Legs   — 2 brown cock hackles

LARGE RED SEDGE (Murrough Fly)
Hook   — size 8-10 dry-fly
Body   — claret dubbing, ribbed gold oval
Hackles   — 1. red game cock, palmered
                   2. ditto at throat
Wing   — as for Hoolet

Note: body dubbing may also be wound over a buoyant material like cork to use this pattern as a wake-fly
Antennae are probably unnecessary on most sedge imitations, but a pair of stripped cree cock hackle stalks may be tied-in, under the wings, then divided to slope forward in front of the hook eye.

Mayflies

TAYLOR'S GREEN CHAMPION (Dun)

Hook	— sizes 8-10 mayfly
Tail	— three strands of either silver or golden pheasant tail
Body	— apple green floss silk, ribbed black button-thread
Hackles	— 1. badger cock, shortish, palmered 2. badger cock at throat with a turn or two of olive cock in front
Wings	— two brown partridge hackles, dyed green drake, tied forward over hook eye, with narrow splay

Taylor's Yellow Champion is dressed in similar style, substituting the green body floss for yellow, and with the wings dyed yellow drake.

SPENT BLACK DRAKE (Male Spinner)

This was my own pattern for the Test and Anton

Hook	— sizes 10 or 12 mayfly
Tail	— three strands of Golden Pheasant Tail
Body	— fluo-white floss, ribbed black button-thread, and in the opposite direction, with fine scarlet fluo floss
Wings	— four black cock hackle points, tied 'spent', two on each side
Hackle	— short badger cock

'SKINHEAD' MINI-MUDDLER (For 'wind-drift' fishing)

Hook	— size 12-14
Body	— (choice of colour) body floss
Head	— fine bucktail, tied Muddler style and close cropped

Note: this fly is designed to drift in the wind on a bellied-line in buzzer hatches.

Suitable colours for bodies are: black, white, olive, orange with silver rib, red, and fluo if desired.

SILVERHORN (Grouse Tail)

Hook	— size 12 dry-fly
Body	— olive tying thread, ribbed fine round gold tinsel
Hackles	— 1. Furnace cock, palmered 2. ditto at head

Antennae   — two stripped grizzle cock hackle stalks, tied under wing and separated to point forwards in front of hook-eye

Wing   — strip of speckled grouse tail feather, tied flat and folded over hook shank.

Note: the antennae of this pattern are distinctive and add to its attraction

TERRY'S TERROR (General attractor)

Hook   — size 12-14 dry-fly

Tail   — mixed fibres of orange and yellow cock hackles, clipped short

Body   — bronze peacock herl, ribbed fine flat copper lurex

Hackle   — rich, dark red cock.

Note: this is Dr Terry's standard fly, but I have substituted cock hackle fibres for the tail, replacing the usual hair, to lighten the fly.

FLOATING SHRIMP

Finally, I describe my strangest dry-fly, the floating shrimp. This is the standard nymph dressing, but tied with a stiff olive body hackle to replace the softer hen. It is well greased to make if float, and against all of the rules of common sense and nature, I've caught many fish on the Test when they were heads-down in the weed beds, flushing out shrimps. They followed the fly downstream and captured the apparently unnatural escapee . . . strange, but true.

Nymphs

CORIXA (Water Boatman)

Hook sizes	— 8 to 14
Body	— built up with white fluo floss, covered with pearl lurex and ribbed with brown button-thread. May be weighted with a layer of fine lead wire.
Back	— six or eight strands of cock pheasant tail, laid over back from hook bend, then varnished. Divided into two sections on either side of hook for the paddles.

FOOTBALLER SERIES (Chironomid Pupa)

Hook	— 8 to 16, shrimp type or wet-fly
Tail	— white fluo floss, tied round bend to point downwards
Body	— black and white stripped cock hackle stalks wound side by side along hook shank from half way round the hook bend.
Thorax	— light ginger fur from hare's mask
Head	— peacock herl
Breathing tubes	— tuft of white fluo floss taken upwards between the head and thorax

Coloured versions, green, olive, red, orange, claret, brown etc are made by substituting the black hackle stalk for one of the chosen colour, remainder of the dressing unchanged. The black version uses just the black stalk.

Dry-Fly version adds two glassy light blue dun cock hackle points, sloping backwards after thorax, but leaving out the breathing tubes. Badger cock hackle.

The emerger version leaves out the wings and the badger hackle is clipped very short. The dry-fly and emerger patterns can also be in various colours. If supple horsehair can be found, this makes for an alternative body material, with fine segmented effect.

GOOD NEWS NYMPH (Sedge Pupa)

Hook	— standard long shank size 8 to 12
Body	— the lower half is weighted with one layer of fine lead wire. Over this is dubbed a mixture of dyed furs or man-made fibres in yellow, amber, red and a few strands of blue for an overall amberish effect. This is ribbed with gold oval tinsel.
Head	— peacock herl

The half-body weighting is very important in this pattern for its posture in the water.

HOGLOUSE

Hook	— sizes 10 and 12, weighted
Hackle	— grey partridge, divided at rear of hook
Body	— greyish natural rabbit's fur ribbed silver oval tinsel

JACK KETCH (Water beetle)

Hook	— sizes 8 to 12 standard wet-fly
Tag	— flat silver tinsel for air bubble effect
Body	— two layers of fine lead wire, built up in middle. Mixed dubbing over, of black, blue and a few strands of crimson for overall blackish effect. No rib.
Hackle	— long black hen, two turns over, or the spade black hackle from natural red cock cape.

TWO-TONE NYMPHS

Primarily designed for upstream fishing on fast water, they suit all river and lake conditions. The aim in dressing is to achieve a tone-contrast between abdomen and thorax.

HARE'S EAR (March Brown)

Hook	— size 12, medium-long shank
Body	— light brown fur from hare's mask, ribbed fine round gold tinsel or fine yellow fluo floss
Thorax	— dark brown fur from hare's ear over a few turns of fine lead wire
Wing Case	— a strip of brown hen primary wing feather.

IRON BLUE

Hook	— size 16 medium-long shank
Body	— mole's fur dubbed onto crimson thread, ribbed fine copper wire
Thorax	— claret dubbing over fine lead wire
Wing Case	— strip of waterhen or coot primary

LARGE DARK OLIVE (Blue Dun)

Hook	— size 12 medium-long shank
Body	— blue dun herl ribbed with fine lime fluo floss
Thorax	— dark olive dubbing over fine lead wire
Wing Case	— strip of grey duck primary wing feather

MEDIUM OLIVE

As above, but with contrasting shades of medium olive herl for the abdomen, ribbed fine gold round tinsel and dark olive dubbing for the thorax

PALE WATERY

As above, but using contrasting pale olive herl for the abdomen and medium olive dubbing for the thorax.

PHEASANT TAIL

Hook	— 14 and 12, medium-long shank
Body	— reddish cock pheasant centre tail, ribbed copper wire
Thorax	— bright copper wire, built up and pheasant tail herls over for wing case

Wet Flies

Author's note: I have not put my name to the patterns listed in this appendix. Some, the Footballer and Jack Ketch, are original patterns of mine. Others are adaptions and variations of standard patterns, which, in my experience, improve their fish-catching potential. This adaption is one of the pleasures of our fly-fishing sport but we should never forget the tribute we owe to the originator, or to long-lost tradition.

BLUE DUN (Large Dark Olive)

Hook	— Wet-fly, sizes 10 and 12
Body	— blue mole's fur, ribbed with a strand of fine lime fluo floss
Hackle	— blue dun cock
Wing	— grey mallard primary, or coot or waterhen for darker version

BROUGHTON POINT (Iron Blue Dun)

Hook	— Wet-fly, size 12-16
Body	— Purple floss silk
Hackle	— Black cock with a few fibres of dyed red cock in front
Wing	— starling primary

An alternative body colour is to mix claret and red dubbing (Mulberry). Both patterns can be winged with coot or waterhen for a darker pattern

DARK CLARET and GROUSE

Hook	— Wet-fly, sizes 8-16
Tail	— tippet
Body	— claret dubbing mixed with mole's fur, ribbed fine round gold tinsel
Hackle	— light red game cock
Wing	— well marked speckled grouse tail

The mixture of the two dubbings gives better effect than plain dark claret.

KATE MacLAREN (Heather Fly version)

Hook	— Wet-fly, sizes 8-14
Tail	— Topping
Body	— black dubbing, cross ribbed with fine scarlet fluo floss, reverse direction. Fine round silver ribbing over hackle
Hackle	— 1. black cock, palmered 2. natural red game cock at head

APPENDIX – SPECIAL FLY PATTERNS

BLOODY KATE (Bob-fly version of above for use in heavy wave)

Hook	— Wet-fly, sizes 6-12
Tail	— topping
Body	— bottom half, scarlet fluo floss, top half, black dubbing
Ribbing	— fine round silver tinsel over both sections
Hackles	— 1. black cock over black dubbing only 2. red game cock at head

MARCH BROWN

Hook	— Wet-fly, sizes 10-14
Body	— light brown hare's ear, ribbed with strand of fine yellow fluo floss
Hackle	— brown partridge or cree cock
Wing	— speckled partridge tail or well-marked hen pheasant primary

PEARLY INVICTA

Hook	— Wet-fly, sizes 10-14
Tail	— topping
Body	— two layers of fine pearl lurex over bright flat silver tinsel or lurex
Hackle	— pinch of blue jay
Wing	— hen pheasant primary

SPIDER PATTERNS (for North Country and rain-fed rivers)

Note: it is not my intention to describe all of the traditional, well-documented patterns. The description is to differentiate between dressing styles for downstream and upstream fishing.

DOWNSTREAM — the aim is to make a slim body of the chosen colour, from the natural silk tying thread itself, very fine body floss or dubbing fur very thinly spun. The chosen game-bird or poultry hackle is then wound on at the head and coned backwards with turns of thread to partly mask the body of the fly.

UPSTREAM — the materials are the same, but after the hackle has been wound, it is pulled forwards towards the hook eye and bolstered by turns of thread behind. The whip finish is made behind the hackle so that the fibres stand out proudly from the hook shank. Fibres may be stripped from one side of the hackle stalk for a sparser dressing which is more lively in the water.

Variation in shade of hackle is obtained by having darker fibres from the outside of a bird's neck or wing, and the lighter inside.

Thus snipe and woodcock offer two options of hackle colour for the chosen body colour, viz: Dark snipe and purple, light snipe and purple. Hook sizes are small, 12 to 16, but never forget that wire thickness can be chosen to fish at various depths, or to suit the speed of the flow.

SWEENY VARIANTS

These killing flies are based on Richard Walker's famous Sweeny Todd reservoir lure. The aim is to offer colour variations, but within a wet-fly format.

Hook	— Wet-fly, sizes 10 and 12
Body	— first half, black floss ribbed fine round silver. Second half of any chosen fluorescent colour: red, lime, yellow, orange, magenta, or pearl lurex over white fluo floss
Hackle	— to match the fluo floss
Wing	— fairly sparse black bucktail.

Dapping Flies

HORNED DADDY (Crane Fly)

Hook	— sizes 6 and 8 wet-fly or Wilson
Body	— brown midge floss, oiled or greased
Rib	— fine oval gold tinsel
Hackles	— red game, palmered, then two more wound thickly at head, leaving longish hackle points above the hook to catch the wind to make the fly skate.

OLIVE DRAKE (Mayfly Dun for large lakes)

Hook	— sizes 6-10 wet-fly or Wilson
Tail	— Tippet, tied thickly
Body	— Olive dubbing, ribbed oval gold tinsel
Hackles	— 1. Olive cock, palmered
	2. Olive cock at throat, blue guinea fowl in front

SILVER BLUE (Attractor for salmon and sea trout)

Hook	— sizes 6 and 8 wet-fly, or Wilson
Body	— first half flat silver, second half blue dubbing, ribbed oval silver
Hackles	— 1. Bright blue cock over blue dubbing only, tightly wound.
	2. Grizzle or badger cock as bushy collar at head.

Fly dressing details: I have deliberately excluded tail fibres from stream wet-flies and nymphs as experience proves them unnecessary. Matching hackle fibres can be added if desired. In most cases the colour of the tying silk is unimportant as fluo ribbing replaces the older concept of the silk 'shining through' the dubbing.

The same fluo ribbings are used on spider versions of the Blue Dun and March Brown.

Salmon and Sea Trout Flies

HAIR WING BLACK DOCTOR (Brush Off System)

Hook	— usually tied on large singles, sizes 2-3/0
Tag	— round silver tinsel and yellow floss
Tail	— topping
Butt	— bright red wool, repeated at head
Body	— Black floss, ribbed flat silver tinsel
Hackles	— 1. blue cock, doubled and wound up body behind tinsel
	2. blue guinea fowl at throat
Wings	— blue, red, yellow bucktail with brown over.
Cheeks	— jungle cock, optional.

Brush off nylon approx 8-10 lb. b.s. tied in at butt and looped around bend to mask point and tied in at throat before hackle and wing is made.

With care, the brush off system can be applied to reasonably sized doubles.

COLLIE DOG

Hook	— size 8-12 double
Body	— silver lurex closely ribbed with silver oval tinsel
Wings	— long strands from a black calf tail which must have a pronounced curl.

The use of a small double balances the fly.

HUSBAND'S SHRIMP

Hook	— double salmon irons, sizes 2-8
Hackles (legs)	— two very long brown cock hackles wound round bend to trail behind, then palmered up body to be clipped short.
Body	— brown floss silk, whole body soaked in cellulose varnish.

MOONLIGHT ON MRS HIGGINGBOTHAM

(Simplified version of J. D. Greenway's pattern, an excellent fly for night fishing for sea trout)

Hook	— sizes 6-12 wet-fly.
Tail	— G.P. topping
Body	— black dubbing
Rib	— oval silver tinsel
Hackle	— natural guinea fowl
Wing	— black and white barred silver pheasant wing secondary feather.

166

PURPY
(Modern tube fly version of an old Spey fly. This killed a 32lb fish at Melrose)

Tube	— alloy or brass 1"-2"
Body	— purple floss silk, ribbed with gold tinsel and yellow floss
Wing	— bunches of purple and yellow bucktail alternating.

SILVER DOCTOR HACKLE-POINT WING

Hook	— ordinary forged salmon iron
Tag	— round silver tinsel and yellow floss.
Tail	— G.P. topping
Butt	— scarlet wool
Body	— flat silver tinsel or lurex ribbed fine silver oval
Hackles	— 1. Blue cock, palmered and doubled 2. Barred teal at throat
Wing	— Pairs of hackle points, scarlet, blue and yellow over tippet strands; teal and crest over.
Head	— scarlet wool, red varnished head.

THUNDER and LIGHTNING SHEATH WING
Combines hair and feather

Hook	— salmon irons, single or double
Tag	— round gold tinsel and yellow floss
Tail	— topping
Butt	— black ostrich herl
Body	— black floss, ribbed with flat gold and narrow oval gold tinsels
Hackles	— 1. Orange cock, doubled and palmered up the body 2. Blue guinea fowl at throat
Wing	— bunch of brown squirrel tail sheathed over with strips of brown mallard with jungle cock cheeks either side G.P. crest over.

WHAUP and SILVER

Hook	— sizes 6 and 8 wet-fly
Tail	— tippet
Body	— silver flat tinsel, ribbed silver oval
Hackle	— black hen
Wings	— Curlew primary. Note Curlew is on the list of protected species, but a lightish woodcock primary, or seagull is a substitute.

Whaup and Yellow is the same dressing above, but with yellow wool body ribbed with oval gold, and light ginger hackle.

Night fishing fly is shown with a nylon loop whipped to hook shank for easy changing in the dark. The nylon should be crimped before tying down. Fly is blue and silver with silver pheasant wing instead of teal.

New Wine in Old Bottles

Not only did Kelson hi-jack a large number of other men's flies and ideas, but he played a large part in the over-complication of salmon fly-dressing. A century earlier anglers were wise and took their fish with simpler structures. Happily, we have reverted to the former simplicities, with hair-wings, Waddingtons and tube flies.

Had it not been for Kelson and his ilk, the patterns used by Scrope on the Tweed would have come down to us. I attempted to revive the old eighteenth century flies by converting them into modern tube fly patterns, and they do catch fish. I keep Scrope's entrancing fly-names.

I remain faithful to the original colours though obviously with modern materials.

Although Toppy was the best known, the best killer is probably Michael Scott.

KINMONT WILLIE
Mount — choice of tube or Waddington shank
Body — in three sections, red, brown, yellow, floss or dubbing, with gold tinsel rib
Collar — black bucktail and teal fibres

LADY OF MERTOUN
Mount — as above
Body — in three sections, yellow, blue dun and red, with silver rib
Collar — grey squirrel, dyed yellow

MEG WITH THE MUCKLE MOUTH
Mount — as above
Body — in three sections, yellow, red, yellow with gold rib
Collar — brown squirrel

MEG IN HER BRAWS
Mount — as above
Body — in three sections, yellow, brown, yellow with gold rib
Collar — brown squirrel

MICHAEL SCOTT
Mount — as above
Body — in three sections, yellow, black and yellow, with silver rib
Collar — black and natural bucktail

TOPPY

Mount	— as above
Body	— in three sections, yellow, black and red, silver rib
Collar	— black bucktail with teal fibres.

THE LITTLE INKY BOY

I give below, for historical interest the dressing of this fly in George Kelson's own words, culled from his letter in the 26 October issue of the *Fishing Gazette* in 1907. I doubt anyone would want to dress it today, but it marks the final absurdity of the complex salmon fly, and the start of its long-drawn out demise. It lead to the death of Kelson's reputation in his own life time (see text).

Tag	— silver twist and two turns of crimson Berlin wool
Tail	— a topping, a point of the tippet imitation of the Querula Cruenta and a narrow strip of summer duck
Butt	— black herl
Body	— thick black horsehair, closely coiled
Hackle	— from the centre of body of tourocou crest
Throat	— a buttercup yellow furnace hackle
Wings	— G.P. tippet in strands, unbarred Mandarin drake a right and left hand claret strand of tourocou two narrow strips of summer duck, a suspicion of gallena and a topping.

LURES

I have no prejudice against lures, which are nothing more than large wet-flies, based on the American families of streamers and bucktails. I have invented two, the Beastie types which have weighted heads, and one variation of the Gray Ghost, Mrs. Carrie Steven's effective streamer. I have given this an olive-green 'back' to copy roach and rudd fry for British conditions.

BEASTIE

Hook	— size 6 long shank lure hook
Body	— black floss silk, ribbed flat silver
Hackle and underwing	— bunches of hot orange marabou feather
Wing	— two black marabou plumes tied back to back to extend well beyond the hook bend
Cheeks	— barred silver pheasant flank feathers tied on either side of the hook shank, the central stalks level with the shank. Jungle cock eyes over if desired.

| Head | — about 6 mms of lead wire in two layers, varnish or superglue and covered with black thread. Head painted to taste. |

A white version substitutes white marabou for the main wings, with fluo pink marabou feather for the hackle and underwing.

VOODOO

The structure of the Voodoo lure is the same as the beastie, but it uses combinations of fluo marabou for the hackle, underwings and main wings. A killing version uses fluo lime green for the hackle and underwing and hot orange marabou plumes for the main wing.

OLIVE GHOST (Roach and rudd fry)

Hook	— size 6 long shanked lure hook
Body	— orange floss, ribbed flat silver tinsel
Hackle	— four strands of bronze peacock herl with a small bunch of white marabou feather, both extending slightly beyond hook bend. Under these is a long G.P. crest feather, curving upwards
Wing	— two pairs of olive cock hackles, tied streamer fashion, extending well beyond hook bend, with a G.P. topping over
Cheeks	— a pair of silver pheasant flank feathers, jungle cock over
Head	— this is fairly long, finished with white varnish and a band of red in the middle.

These lures are meant for rainbow trout in waters where they feed on fry, Grafham, Rutland, Hanningfield for example. They have also been effective against pike (with short wire trace) and also big catches of mullet have been made on Beasties in Christchurch harbour.

I have also used silver and black versions of the Jersey Herd, and the same structure of the J.H. with green and brown ostrich herl body for stickle-backing trout in dull-water conditions when the bait fish appear to be drab.

GREEN and BROWN JERSEY (Drab Minnow)

Hook	— size 6 or 8 long shank lure hook
Tail and back	— eight strands bronze peacock herl
Body	— green and brown ostrich herl, wound side by side, over brown floss under body ribbed gold oval
Hackle	— olive cock, doubled
Head	— the peacock herl, twisted and wound

Bibliography

Balfour-Kinnear, G.P.R.: *Flying Salmon* (1937)
Bates, Joe: *Atlantic Salmon Flies & Fishing* (1970)
Behrendt, Alex: *The Management of Angling Waters* (1977)
Bluett, J.: *Sea Trout and Occasional Salmon* (1948)
Clapham, Brian: *Fishing Moorland Becks*
Crawford, Lesley: *Caithness & Sutherland Trout Loch Country* (1990)
Crossley, Anthony: *Floating Line for Salmon & Sea Trout*
Francis, Francis: *Book on Angling* (1867)
Gray, L.R.N. ('Lemon Grey'): *Torridge Fishery*
Greene, H. Plunket: *Where the Bright Waters Meet* (1927)
Greenway, J.D.: *Fish, Fowl and Foreign Lands*
Grey, Sir Edward: *Fly Fishing* (1899)
Halford, F.M.: *An Angler's Autobiography* (1903)
Harris, J.R.: *An Angler's Entomology* (1952)
Hidy, V.S.: *The Pleasures of Fly Fishing* (1972)
Hills, J.W.: *River Keeper* (1934)
Houghton: *Chronicles of the Houghton Fishing Club* (1822-1908)
Hutton, J. Arthur: *Salmon Fishing on the Wye* (1930)
Ivens, T.C.: *Still Water Fly Fishing* (1952)
Kelson, Geo. M.: *The Salmon Fly* (1895)
Macan & Worthington: *Life in Lakes and Rivers* (1959)
Mackintosh, Alexander: *The Modern Fisher or Driffield Angler* (1806)
Marston, R.B.: *The Fishing Gazettes* (Editor)
'North Country Angler': *The Art of Angling* (1800)
Pequegnot, Jean-Paul: *Repertoire des Mouches Artificielles Françaises* (1984)
Pritt, T.E.: *North Country Flies* (1885)
Pulman, G.P.R.: *The Vade Mecum of Fishing* (1841)
Ransome, Arthur: *Rod and Line*

Sawyer, Frank: *Nymphs and the Trout*
Scrope, Wm.: *Days & Nights of Salmon Fishing in the Tweed* (1843)
Stewart, W.C.: *The Practical Angler* (1857)
Walker, C.F.: *Lakes Flies and their Imitation* (1960)
Wanless, Alexander: *Threadline Questions Answered* (1931)
Williams, A. Courtney: *A Dictionary of Trout Flies*

Index